MUSIC PRODUCTION METHODS

music**PRO** guides

MUSIC PRODUCTION METHODS

A Concise Guide for Understanding Your Role, Process, and Order

Josh Bess

ROWMAN & LITTLEFIELD
Lanham • Boulder • New York • London

Published by Rowman & Littlefield
An imprint of The Rowman & Littlefield Publishing Group, Inc.
4501 Forbes Boulevard, Suite 200, Lanham, Maryland 20706
www.rowman.com

6 Tinworth Street, London SE11 5AL, United Kingdom

British Library Cataloguing in Publication Information Available

Library of Congress Cataloging-in-Publication Data

Names: Bess, Josh, author.
Title: Music production methods : a concise guide for understanding your
  role, process, and order / Josh Bess.
Description: Lanham : Rowman & Littlefield, 2021. | Series: Music pro
  guides | Includes index. | Summary: "Josh Bess provides a concise and
  accessible guide to music production and the role of a producer,
  breaking it down into core concepts, approaches, and methods essential
  to any piece of recorded music regardless of style or genre. Music
  Production Methods will help producers troubleshoot workflows and
  ultimately create better music"— Provided by publisher.
Identifiers: LCCN 2021018764 (print) | LCCN 2021018765 (ebook) | ISBN
  9781538156254 (cloth) | ISBN 9781538156261 (paperback) | ISBN
  9781538156278 (epub)
Subjects: LCSH: Sound recordings—Production and direction. | Popular
  music—Production and direction.
Classification: LCC ML3790 .B397 2021 (print) | LCC ML3790 (ebook) |
  DDC 781.49—dc23
LC record available at https://lccn.loc.gov/2021018764
LC ebook record available at https://lccn.loc.gov/2021018765

CONTENTS

ABOUT THE MEDIA CONTENT

Throughout this book, the author uses exercise prompts to increase engagement and practice through active learning. These exercise templates can be downloaded in PDF format.

You can download a free PDF containing all these images from https://textbooks.rowman.com/bess.

To access these exercise templates, please visit https://textbooks.rowman.com/bess.

INTRODUCTION

Welcome to *Music Production Methods*, a guide to producing music and achieving your goals through planned action. In this book you'll learn not only how to complete the exercises provided, but also how to use them as tools to develop and complete your own productions, no matter your skill level, experience, or genre of choice.

WHO IS THIS BOOK FOR?

This book teaches what many professional producers experience throughout years of practice, education, mentorship, and trial and error, packed into a concise guide that showcases the role of a producer. It breaks down key concepts, approaches, and methods to produce music recordings. I was not fortunate enough to read any guides when beginning my journey as a producer, as there wasn't much educational content out there at the time aside from pure mentorship in the real world of practice. The real-world experiences that I share in this book span the past fifteen years, and are divided into real-life stories in each chapter to incorporate into your own learning. These are stories I wish I could have read from producers who were above my own experience level when I was starting out, as they would have considerably reduced the amount of time it took to enhance the way I produce projects.

These fifteen years begin from my perspective as a musician in a band, to a producer of internationally acclaimed high-scale music projects, leading to my role as a teacher of music production, and paying it forward to the up-and-coming generation of aspiring producers. As a teacher, I quickly learned that there was a need for this book; it all starts with a single question that I ask all of my students: "What is a music producer?" The wide range of answers is the reason for this book; I have learned that many of my students are either unaware of what a music producer is—or even better, they present a "correct" answer to this question, very different from their peers. This book answers this question along with exposing readers to the philosophy and the vagueness of this role, a topic that is rarely confronted by students of music and audio production.

- This book is for students of music production who seek clarification of the role they are aspiring to take on.
- This book is for experienced producers who may have a great grasp of the creative outlook on production, although have never received formal training on the subject.
- This book is for producers, both novice and experienced, who are hitting roadblocks in their workflow and need a boost of encouragement from proven methods and exercises.
- This book is for the bedroom producers at home on their laptops and looking for a new way to create, all the way to studio professionals looking for a way to manage their team.
- This book is for any and all producers of music recordings of any genre, hoping to gain a formal understanding of the trade and art form of music production.

WHAT IS *MUSIC PRODUCTION METHODS* ALL ABOUT?

The purpose of this book is to introduce three main concepts of music production:

1. The role of a music producer
2. The process of recorded music
3. The order of the music production process

These three concepts are essential to any piece of recorded music, any genre, or any style of music; both the novice-level producer and the experienced producer will greatly benefit from understanding these concepts. This is important to understand, as the role of a producer is constantly evolving in relation to music, time, and technological transitions and updates. This book allows both aspiring and experienced producers to understand that throughout these changes, there are proven similarities within all musical productions regarding workflow management and understanding. This is a book that is designed to age well, and to be used as a tool for personal and institutional learning.

WHAT IF I DON'T PRODUCE MUSIC?

Music Production Methods, as an instructional guide for producing music, teaches you how to produce music without requiring music or production experience, let alone any knowledge of music thus far. The exercises show you exactly how to think about and plan your production workflow. For those who already produce music, understand song writing, sound design, recording, mixing, and technology involved with a production, your knowledge will definitely help your understanding of this book, although it is not a prerequisite. Throughout this book, I provide detailed explanations of every process, including the names, background, and context of when these processes are used.

So once again, don't worry if you are not familiar with music production; you'll still be able to use this book. By reading each chapter, moving forward with each exercise, and referring to the text, you will come naturally to understanding the language of music production, even if it's foreign to you now—it will be easier than you believe.

THE METHODOLOGY

The biggest problem that most music producers have isn't starting an amazing song or production; it's actually finishing it. Every year, tens of thousands of music creators start and quit because they don't understand this one essential skill: the art and science of production. This book guides you through eight methods that are essential for a producer to understand in order to eliminate roadblocks and complete projects, all explained through real-life stories and experiences to not only teach you the methods, but share true context as well. Each chapter is broken down in the following manner:

1. The story of my professional experience
2. Principles taken from this experience
3. The story of teaching these principles
4. An exercise for your own application

The first three methods guide you through the fundamentals of music production:

Method #1—Understand Your Role: Understand the role of a producer and take command of your goals.

Method #2—Understand Your Process: Understand the process of music production and determine the elements you need to move your projects forward.

Method #3—Understand Your Order: Understand the order of your process and advance your projects efficiently from start to finish.

The next three methods guide you through an in-depth perspective on music production:

Method #4—Song Writing and Arranging: Understand key elements and resources for telling a story through your production.

Method #5—Sound Design and Recording: Understand key elements and resources for designing and documenting the emotion of your production.

Method #6—Mixing and Mastering: Understand key elements and recourses for balancing the sonic qualities of your production.

The final two methods guide you on a path of reflection and development of your own production experience, skills, and knowledge.

Method #7—Modern Problems and Solutions: Understand where problems are occurring and proceed toward your goals with solutions.

Method #8—Your Mentor: Understand the power of mentorship and learn priceless lessons of the trade.

By the end of this book you will have an immense number of tools to get started, make progress, and complete music projects at a pace that is not only incredibly efficient, but one that allows you to express your own creativity with a reach greater than your own, through community and teamwork to produce the projects you aspire to undertake.

I

THE FUNDAMENTALS
OF MUSIC PRODUCTION

In this section you will dive into three methods that build the foundation of music production. This is how the methods in this section are laid out:

1. Each method begins with a story of mine, a true personal experience related to the topic and the learning experiences provided.
2. This story then leads to principles to take away from these experiences.
3. This is followed by a personal experience I had with my students, where these principles were applied.
4. Each method concludes with an exercise for you to do to improve your own music production skill set.

❶

UNDERSTAND YOUR ROLE

I distinctly remember my first encounter with an accomplished music producer who I was lucky enough to work with early in my own career (if that's what it could be called at the time) as a drummer for a pop band. The band, which I will not name for now, was doing pretty well at the time, with release upon release used in television commercials and other sync work coming from the likes of Nickelodeon, Disney Channel, MTV, and many other networks. The production of each of these songs that wound up placed on these networks followed a very similar process, and these were *all* constructed and supervised from a birds-eye view by a very specific person: a music producer. Here's how it all began.

About ten years ago, I was invited to play drums with an up-and-coming artist in a private rehearsal studio in New York City, to perform a song for a very special music producer who was in town and interested in working with this particular artist. At the time, I had no idea what a producer would even do with an artist or band. I simply believed that "good things will happen," for no apparent reason other than in direct relation to their portfolio of success; this was enough to be excited about at the time. It was time to showcase our music for this producer, and he arrived, took a seat in front of the band in the rehearsal room, and we performed the song. While performing, I was watching the producer.

He was sitting there with his eyes closed, and I didn't really understand what he was doing, although I knew he was listening. At the time I didn't know *what* he was listening to, although I now understand that strong intent to listen to *everything*. He was listening at a level I couldn't even imagine at the time. He was listening to every pluck of the guitar, every beat of the drum; he noticed every lyric the singer sang, and overall, he noticed the emotion of the music and how well we were, or *were not,* communicating this emotion. He had a skill set that I could not even begin to understand, and he was easily able to communicate what we needed to adjust, how we needed to adjust these things, and why we needed to do so.

This producer ended up working with our group, and this led to many recording sessions and song placements that shared our music with the world at a level I couldn't have imagined before meeting this incredible person. I can recall one question that I asked this producer, and his answer changed the way I looked at music, and the role I would soon aspire to take on. My somewhat inadequate question was simple: "How did you get all of these songs placed on TV shows?" And his answer was even more simple: "This was the goal from the beginning." To be honest, it wasn't quite the answer I was looking for, though now it makes more sense than ever. It makes sense because he was so sure about every decision made through the end of production. He knew what the end result would be; he knew [what] the end goal was, how to reach that goal, and most important, what his own role was in the entire process. This was the moment I became intrigued not only by this person, but by this *role*, and I knew diving into music production was something worth doing.

PRINCIPLES

Music producers need to *understand their role* better than anyone else. A common issue among even experienced music producers is a lack of understanding of their own role in a music project. If you find yourself in this boat, don't be discouraged; the role of a music producer is often difficult to grasp, as this role is constantly adjusting with updated approaches to music creation. I'll start off by saying that a music producer is essential to the production of any documented music; but that being said, the role is bound to undergo changes because the overall creation and documentation of music since the late 1800s have definitely experienced a few updates—to say the least—to arrive at where music is now. Yet, even throughout the ever-changing process of music production as we know it, the music producer has always kept one essential role intact; to understand this role, let's discuss two essential words that define the art and science of music production.

Production: The act of creation.
Producer: The person who exercises general supervision of a production.

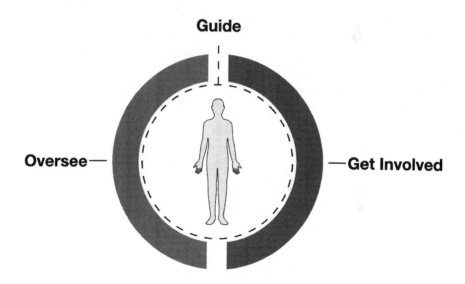

Simply put, the producer will *guide* the production *process*, and the producer has two main options to move forward with this guidance:

1. The producer will *solely guide* and oversee the process of the music production, or;
2. The producer will guide the process of the music production, while *being involved* with the process.

To get a full-scale explanation and detailed examination of this description, let's take a look at the Recording Academy's "GRAMMY Award Eligible Credit Definitions" for the title of producer.

Producer: The producer is the primary person who directs, and has overall creative and technical oversight of, the entire recording project and the individual recording sessions that are a part of the project. The producer participates in and/or supervises the recording session and works directly with the artist, musicians, and engineers. He or she makes creative, technical, and aesthetic decisions that realize the goals of both the artist and the sound recording copyright owner in the creation of musical content. The producer may perform, direct performances, choose final takes or versions, and oversee the selection of songs, musicians, singers, arrangers, studios, etc. The producer, in collaboration with the artist, assigns credits to performers and technical personnel and is responsible for supplying accurate crediting information to the record label or media company as official documentation. Other duties of the producer may include, but are not limited to, overseeing other staffing needs, keeping budgets and schedules, adhering to deadlines, supervising mastering, and overall quality control.

Producer
GRAMMY® Award Eligible Credit Definitions

Based on this definition, here are four main takeaways:

1. Guidance
2. Taste

3. Understanding
4. Involvement

Guidance

He or she makes creative, technical and aesthetic decisions that realize the goals of both the artist and the sound recording.

—"GRAMMY Award Eligible Credit Definitions"
for the title of producer

A common misconception regarding the producer's role in a music project is that the producer *must* be physically involved with the production;
this could be imagined as writing a song, recording a musician's work,
sound designing a synth, mixing, or engineering, although this is not
true. A producer's guiding role may take the form of oversight, management, or even consultation.

So, the big question here is, "*What* exactly does the producer guide?"
This, however, may not be the right question; let's ask, "*Who* does
the producer guide?" A producer guides a group or individual (this
individual can also be the producer him or herself) through the music
production process, with the goal of achieving an output of music. This
may not sound like much from the outside, but it is an incredibly useful
and important role to take on.

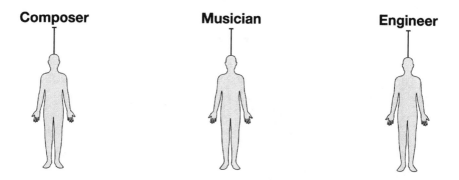

Composer   **Musician**   **Engineer**

A musical artist, a musician, a recording engineer, and a mixing engineer, all have a common end goal, but have very different roles in

the process to achieve this shared goal. A producer who understands each individual role and guides each role to the next step is very helpful because each person in the process can fully concentrate on his or her role without worrying about what's coming next or what's missing. The producer takes the pressure off everyone throughout the production process, allowing the people involved to focus their time, creativity, and effort on their own given tasks.

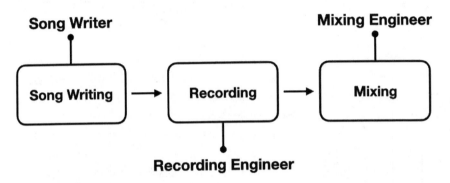

In short, the producer creates an environment that encourages performance and achievement. This is done through arguably the most important characteristic (aside from experience, creativity, and efficiency). This is *taste*.

Taste

Tasteful: Showing good aesthetic judgment or appropriate behavior.

As you'll learn throughout this book, tasteful decisions may include choosing a music composition; choosing an emotional feel for an instrument; choosing not only the "best" mixing engineer, but the "most fitting" mixing engineer for a specific project—all leading to music produced through the experience, knowledge, and taste of the producer. There are many producers in the world who take on this overseer role. It is not only incredibly helpful, but also incredibly rare, difficult, and requires a specific type of person who can combine the many aspects of emotion, strategy, sensitivity, patience, command, and likability, to work with anyone from a child in his or her bedroom to accomplished artists, composers, sound designers, and engineers in the studio to produce a final musical work.

Understanding Your Tasks

> The producer participates in and/or supervises the recording session and works directly with the artist, musicians, and engineers.
>
> —"GRAMMY Award Eligible Credit Definitions"
> for the title of producer

Music producers guide both the music and engineering process as either supervisors or as musicians and/or engineers themselves. This means that a producer equipped with knowledge and experience of both music composition and engineering will have a greater idea of direction for each of these tasks, whether the producer is participating in the task or guiding somebody else to handle it, allowing for more creative options in the end. It is very similar to a film director who understands not only how to write a script, but how to work a camera, understanding what each camera lens does and how each functions. The more the director knows, the more they can guide somebody else to operate the camera.

Involvement in Your Production

As for getting involved in a production, a producer has two choices:

1. The producer will personally oversee and initiate the process of the music production, or
2. The producer will guide a team or individual through the process of the music production, while being involved with the process.

To get a grasp on which choice may benefit your own production, let's take a look at the pros and cons of each choice.

Pros and Cons of Working on Your Own   As with any art form, holding the power of creative freedom over your entire project is commonly desired, although this is not the *only* reason for the many producers choosing to work on their own. Many aspiring producers and accomplished producers enjoy working on their own, but among the wide range of genres and styles of music, the type of producer who most commonly chooses to work alone is the electronic music producer. To understand this, we must answer two fundamental questions: (1) why electronic music producers are able to work on their own, and; (2) why they feel the *need* to work on their own. If you're a producer of electronic music, then this part is a MUST READ. I'm an electronic music producer myself, so I have great confidence in addressing this. If you're not, keep reading on anyway, as it is incredibly helpful to know whether these elements are influencing your own decision to produce on your own.

So, why do electronic music producers enjoy working on their own?

- Advancements in music technology make it possible for a single person to compose, arrange, sound design, mix, master, and complete various other tasks, not only on a wide range of electronic instruments, but even using a single application (a digital audio workstation or DAW, for example) on a personal computer or smart phone/device.
- I'm not sure where or how we came to this point, but many electronic music producers feel they *need* to do everything on their own. This may stem from a sense of creative self-accomplishment, although most feel they need to compose each note of the song whether using drum machines or MIDI (musical instrument digital interface) editors (more on this in Method #4), sound design every synthesizer in their project without presets (Method #5), or mix and master every song they work on (Method #6), on their own. At this point, the producer is taking on every single piece of the process, and distributing the tasks between themselves and their machines (so in a way this is *technically* not working on your own, but we'll consider machines to be our instruments for philosophical reasons I really don't want to dive into right now).

Now that we have that out of the way, let's break down the pros and cons of working on your own.

Table 1.1. Pros and Cons of Working on Your Own

Pros	Cons
Increased *control*	Limited *resources*
Reduced *miscommunication*	Limited *bandwidth*
Reduced *cost*	Limited *time*

The pros: As shown in table 1.1, by working on your own you immediately increase control, reduce (possibly eliminate) miscommunication with others, and reduce your costs. Simply put, you control the project, you do not need to communicate with anyone but yourself (and your machines), and any financial costs are solely on yourself as a creator, which should be far less than including others in the process. The pros are pretty straightforward, so let's dive into the cons.

The cons: Working on your own sounds great, but there are some drawbacks to this. The main disadvantages are limited resources, limited bandwidth, and limited time. There are other disadvantages, but these three are common drawbacks to working on your own, unless you have superb talents across multiple instruments along with sound design and mixing skills. Unless you were born with these talents, it would take time to develop these skills, adding to another main drawback—*limited time*. In the end, the primary con to working on your own is only having yourself (and your machines) to bring your project to life, which often places limits on your achievement. If you find yourself in this position, don't worry. You'll be able to address many, if not all, of these cons by utilizing a team.

Table 1.2. Pros and Cons of Working with a Team

Pros	Cons
Increased *resources*	Increased *miscommunication*
Increased *bandwidth*	Increased *logistics*
Reduced *time*	Increased *cost*

Pros and Cons of Working with a Team **The pros:** Simply put, when involving a team in music production you can immediately increase your resources, increase your bandwidth, and reduce the time needed to complete a project. Going back to our movie director example, simply imagine a movie director writing, acting, shooting, and editing his or her own movie. The idea of bringing in a team to help with this is so incredibly useful that teamwork is not solely intended for movie directors and music producers, but for anyone guiding a team to achieve results, from people involved in creative production to the CEO of a company. Any of these individuals are able to succeed with the help of their team, and in most cases could not succeed without them.

The cons: Working with a team has some drawbacks as well, and these can immediately lead to increased miscommunication, increased logistics, and increased cost to complete a production. As for logistics and cost, these are bound to increase if you are involving additional team members that require studio fees, recording fees, rehearsal fees, transportation fees, dining fees, accommodation fees, and payments in general. Let's not dive too deep into this, as these logistics and costs may be different for each scenario. So, let's simply leave it at this: if you're working with a team, you will commonly include some type of additional logistics and costs to involve them in the production.

As for *miscommunication*, this can become more complicated, so let's dive deeper into this con. As the extension of talents and resources is absolutely beneficial to a production, a very common roadblock within a production team is *team miscommunication*. Team miscommunication may sound like a simple issue to solve, although it may be difficult to avoid in the first place for many; this applies across a wide range of creative industries where team involvement is required. This is because miscommunication is not entirely based on the communication of words, but the communication of *ideas*. As a producer, is it very important to understand how to communicate ideas to production team members. For example, think about explaining to an instrumentalist how to achieve a specific emotion through his or her performance, explaining to a sound designer how to adjust the tone of an instrument, or explaining to a mixing engineer how to balance a sound to the way you hear it *in your head*. This is not only a common issue for producers, but creatives in general. The role of a producer includes overcoming this common difficulty; here are a few ways to help you achieve this.

- Choose team members who show evidence of what you need; team members who can provide specific references from their own prior experiences, such a portfolio of their credits, performances, or any means of showcasing their work, will not only enhance your communication of ideas, but often lead to achieving the results you are aiming for based on proven results.

- Build an extensive vocabulary; the more options you have to explain your thoughts, the better others may understand you. This can be anything from descriptive and expressive vocabulary, all the way to industry-specific terms and slang.
- Build relationships with your team; the better you understand your team members, the more effectively you can communicate with them.
- Build trust with your team; the better you trust your team, the less communication is needed to achieve your intended goals. This trust is commonly built through achievement as a team. For example, if you have achieved great results with a specific group of individuals for a previous project that is similar to an upcoming project, you know that you can trust the same team for the upcoming project, based on those proven results. On the other hand, this also includes replacing team members who were not able to help with achieving your vision in a previous production.

APPLICATION TO YOUR PRODUCTIONS

This story is applicable to both producers starting out and producers who need to refine their process and distribute their tasks. Take the example of a student of mine, whose goal was to release his first EP by *the end of the summer.* Let's call this student, Chase. Chase had about four months to go, and he had been messing around with electronic music production for a few months prior to setting this goal. He wasn't a fresh beginner, although he had a long way to go in order to produce a project that resembled an incredible reference track that he had shown me. I laid it out to him pretty straight and let him know that he had two paths to move forward with this production if he wanted to complete it by the end of the summer.

1. Produce the project on his own
2. Produce the project with a team

If Chase produces the project on his own, it will not sound like the reference track he presented. It will be possible to hit the target deadline date, although this project will simply be a timestamp of his experience at that moment. If he produces the project with a team, it is very possible to find a team member who excels in the elements that he is lacking, enabling him to hit his deadline along with producing a project with high-quality output.

Chase had a natural talent for song writing and sound design, although he needed additional experience to increase his mixing and mastering abilities. For this reason we decided to bring a mixing and mastering engineer to his production team. At first he saw this as "cheating," although he soon learned that it was the complete opposite. I told him stories from working with incredibly accomplished producers in the past, who didn't play drums on the songs—I played the drums; who didn't sing on the track—the artist sang on the tracks. These producers didn't mix the music either—the mixing engineer handled that. Chase learned that the mixing engineer we brought onto his team has focused solely on this one skill, not only for my student's project but for hundreds of other projects for which his sole role is to balance the mixdown of a song.

Chase ended up achieving his goal, and the inclusion of a team member was an essential piece of this. To reach his goal he trained not only in music production techniques, but critical thinking and planning as well. If there was something he had an issue with, or knew it could not happen within his goal's time frame, he learned that he needed to either resolve it himself or find someone to support him in achieving this goal. Here's an exercise we did together, to make this happen. Whenever Chase was hitting a roadblock in his production workflow, we needed to make a choice between improving his own techniques or involving someone else to handle this role. A factor that played into this was the time frame, a deadline we had to work with, which made the exercise easier to follow. This exercise is focused on:

1. Writing a goal
2. Writing a problem that created a roadblock to that goal
3. Writing two possible routes to fix this problem—either on your own or with a team.

Let me show you a few examples of solving problems through a desire to work on *your own*, or with *a team*.

Goal: I want to release an EP this summer.

1. **Problem:** I don't know anything about music theory.
   a. **Self desire:** I want to learn more about music theory.
   b. **Team desire:** I want to include a song writer on my team.
2. **Problem:** I'm terrible at synthesis sound design.
   a. **Self desire:** I want to learn more about synthesizers.
   b. **Team desire:** I want to include a sound designer on my team.
3. **Problem:** I hate the way my mixes sound.
   a. **Self desire:** I want to learn more about mixing and mastering.
   b. **Team desire:** I want to include a mixing and mastering engineer on my team.

Do you see how different these desires are, even though they are addressing the same problem? As for your goal, this could be anything from *produce a song that makes people dance* to *create a dance music hit* to *produce a classical orchestration*. Whatever your personal goals may be, really hone in on what may block you from achieving those goals, and think about solutions to these roadblocks even if you don't know how to achieve them at the moment. Throughout this book you will learn tips, tricks, and information that will help you return to this exercise and update your answers in relation to your newfound knowledge and experience.

Each of those statements above are conversations that many producers are having in their own minds. While they are examples from my own student's experience, when I actually wrote down the thoughts I was having regarding my own goals, I did three things to understand and find a solution to my problems.

1. I wrote hundreds of phrases that I used to say to myself when I tried to identify and solve my own problems.
2. I looked online for forums, videos, articles, and groups to see how others were solving these same problems.
3. I determined whether I, or a team member, was not only capable of solving my issues, but had a *desire* to solve them.

Exercise

For this exercise, write down at least a dozen things that you are saying or thinking as you face a problem that is creating a roadblock in your production workflow, or something you imagine may become an obstacle in the future. Then, determine whether this is something *you* desire to solve on your own, or a *team member* desires to solve for you. Finally, write what this desire would be. This is something you should be doing every day. I'm always looking for the questions and statements that I am saying or thinking as I decide how to move forward with a production. The truth is that most people—including myself—don't see what the issues are until we stop, think, and reflect on them.

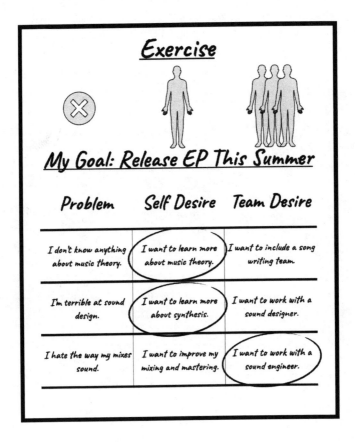

Exercise

My Goal: Release EP This Summer

Problem	Self Desire	Team Desire
I don't know anything about music theory.	I want to learn more about music theory.	I want to include a song writing team.
I'm terrible at sound design.	I want to learn more about synthesis.	I want to work with a sound designer.
I hate the way my mixes sound.	I want to improve my mixing and mastering.	I want to work with a sound engineer.

❷

UNDERSTAND YOUR PROCESS

I am extremely grateful for the opportunities I have had as a musician, as these experiences have offered multiple views into the music production process in ways I could not have imagined. These experiences weren't solely being a musician in a single band; I was involved with different bands and different artists across a wide range of genres, musical styles, and industry platforms—everything from my band when I was a college student playing rooftop and warehouse parties, to rock shows at CBGBs, to pop shows at Irving Plaza, to indie shows at Webster Hall, to jazz sessions at Fat Cat, to the Vans Warped Tour at Nassau Coliseum, to television music placements as a studio drummer. During all these experiences I was able to see not only a specific piece of the process but the *entire* process, meaning everything from the conceptualization of a song to the final performance and recording of the music. And over the span of a few years I learned the most important thing about these processes: they were all *completely different*.

Each and every group or artist I created music with had an incredibly different approach to creating music. Yet as different as each process was, there were elements involved that were *always* the same. This came to me naturally and didn't even appear as a thought, although when I sat down and really dug into the details, it blew my mind to think that every piece of music I have been involved with contained three elements:

1. There was *always* a musical composition, a "song" in some shape or form.
2. There was *always* a way to make this song sound a certain way; we can call this "sound design."
3. There was *always* a way to balance and "mix" all of the instruments to sculpt the listeners' experience.

With every project I worked on, these three elements were always there. The more I thought about it and analyzed it, the more these elements would confirm their existence in every production.

As a musician, I didn't take much note of these elements because I simply focused on my own instrument and what needed to be added to the music from my perspective as a drummer. However, once I began to think about the music from a bird's-eye view—from the perspective of a *producer*—that is when I could confidently take on projects with a clear outlook on not only what the project would sound like, but on each element involved.

PRINCIPLES

Similar to a chef understanding flavor, ingredients, and recipes or a painter understanding color, shape, and texture, a music producer must grasp some essential points in order to develop a deeper understanding of the craft of music production. These points are elements that, when combined, present the production of recorded music. Understanding the existence of these elements will provide you with an incredible foundation for a process for your own productions, and once you know these elements like the back of your hand, you will have endless paths of creativity and countless choices among solutions to problems that may suddenly appear in your path. So, here are the three elements of music production:

- Song writing and arranging
- Sound design and recording
- Mixing and mastering

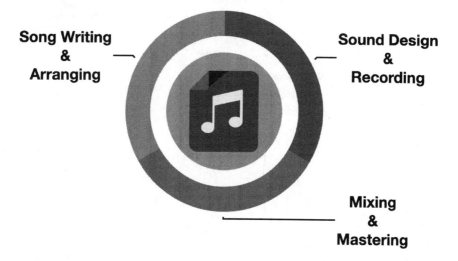

The final production of all music recordings in Western culture will incorporate these three elements, whether the process is intentional or accidental. Simply being aware of this is a humbling discovery not only for aspiring producers, but professional ones as well; music is not only created through impulse, trial and error, or natural talent. Production of music consists of elements that can be combined to produce a planned outcome. Once a student of music production understands the means and functions of each element, the more options that person will have to successfully create, sculpt, and finish music productions. The approach to and action of the process may differ among individuals, and this is the beauty of music production and art creation as a whole; there is no right and no wrong. There is simply creation by intention and creation by accidental discovery; the more you understand, the better you can choose your path, rather than being subject to trial, error, and time.

Song Writing and Arranging

Let's take a look at song writing and arranging, an element of the music production process that is essential—as in no matter the type of music and method of production, this element is part of the process. This element, at its fundamental level, is the act of ordering pitched sounds in musical time and space, most commonly known as a *song*. In Western music, this means choosing a specific note or pitch and deciding when this pitch or group of pitches are produced by a voice or musical instrument. As a music producer, it is advantageous to understand the song creation process, including the options available that generate and conceptualize music. We'll take a deep dive into this in Method #4: "Song Writing and Arranging," but for now let's cover three essential sources that generate a song.

Human   **Electronic**   **Nature**

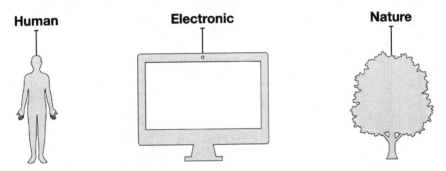

Human   This is fairly straightforward: the act of a person creating music. Rather than focusing on humans as instruments, like slapping a leg or clapping hands, let's focus on the *roles* that a human may play in the music creation process. Two common roles are *composer* and *arranger*. In Method #4, we'll take a closer look at the goals and objectives of these roles.

Electronic   Music is not only created by people, but electronics as well; electronically powered tools such as computers, digital devices, and hardware devices are incredibly useful music composition tools. These can be hardware instruments, software instruments, sequencers, or MIDI effect tools to generate and save music creations. Computers have reached a point where composition and improvisation are possible in relation to the development of technology, namely, randomization tools and artificial intelligence. There are instruments to allow computers to make composition choices and performance choices in reaction to music created by humans. In Method #4, you'll learn why electronic methods are no better or worse than the power of human creation, and just as powerful as your mind allows.

Nature   Before jumping into this one, let me say: Yes, humans are animals, which are technically included in nature, although let's separate the modern human in its own category, as we function somewhat differently than most other animals (e.g., the ability to read this book). So, what is considered *nature*? Nature is the collective phenomena of the physical world, including plants, animals, the landscape, and other features and products of the earth.

Before electronics, and even before human existence, there was life on earth. Most of that life created sound. Animals create sounds to communicate, to search for companions, to warn for danger, to intimidate rivals. Then there are the sounds of gases, liquids, and solids streaming through the world, such as the crashing waves of the ocean and volcanic eruptions. The earth is a life source in constant motion, and this life source is producing sound. For example, when the breeze blows on a tree, the leaves will rustle; this sound is created; this sound is *music*. How the leaves move, how they brush against one another, the length of each movement, the exact frequency and pitches the leaves produce, depend on many components. In Method #4, you'll learn various ways to utilize nature as a source for producing sound for your own music productions.

Sound Design and Recording

The process of sound design and recording is where we design and document the texture and tones of our music. Think of an artist creating a sculpture; the sound design will be where the artist chooses the material for the design of the sculpture, such as wood, concrete, or marble. This is how we design the material of our music composition. And, there are a few ways we can do this.

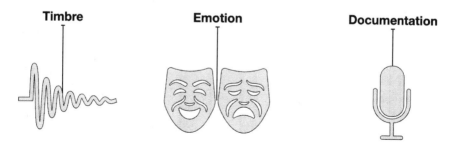

| Timbre | Emotion | Documentation |

Timbre Timbre is essentially *how something sounds*—the perceived sound quality of a pitch, sound, or tone. When we hear a note played on a violin, we know it is a violin; when we hear a piano, we know it is a piano. This is because of the timbre of the note, or what you might call a fingerprint of sound. This is the beauty of sound design, as we can adjust the timbre of any instruments we choose acoustically or electronically. This means that two instruments can play identical pitches, and still produce distinct timbres, distinguishing the *identity* of the instrument to our ears.

Similar to the human aspect of song writing and arranging, there is a human role incorporated into designing the timbre. This ranges anywhere from an instrumentalist controlling the tone of their instrument to a sound designer shaping the tones of synthesized and/or acoustic instruments. In Method #5, "Sound Design and Recording," you will learn a variety of sound design methods and techniques to provide originality and emotional characteristics to a wide range of sound sources. Understanding these roles will allow you as a producer to make choices regarding how to move forward with the adjustment of timbre for a music production.

Emotion   One of the most important interactions and overall takeaways from music is how it affects emotional experience. Music has the ability to cause powerful emotional responses such as chills, thrills, excitement, and sadness. A production of music may alter mood or relieve stress; in everyday life it can be used to regulate, enhance, or diminish undesirable emotional states such as stress, sadness, or anger. Understanding how emotion can be portrayed is essential to the production of music; this is what the listener will feel when interacting with a music recording. Some may argue this is the most important effect of not only music, but art as a whole—to trigger an emotional response. There are many factors in the emotional response to music, anything from musical mimicry to pleasure, all the way to memories.

Music is so much more than notes and pitches, but waves of sound vibrating through the air and ringing through our bodies to create an experience that is stronger than meant for the ears alone, leading the listener's mind and imagination taking the sound even further. A piece of music can bring tears to the listener's eyes, get the body moving and feet tapping, or even activate an anger to the extent that the listener could throw a chair across a room—music is much more powerful than sound alone. The more a music producer understands this power, and develops a sensitivity toward it, the more control the producer has to guide the music toward this emotional goal. As you learned in Method #1: "Understand Your Role," goal setting is an absolute necessity for a production of music, and setting goals based on the delivery of emotional responses is a common practice for many productions.

Documentation Documenting music is more possible than ever in the form of recorded audio. Sound has been recorded since the early 1800s, and although recording has greatly advanced, the concept of engraving sound waves in an analog or digital form of reproduction not only conveys the notes, pitches, and timbre we hear, but the full emotional experience. As a music producer, the understanding of audio recording and engineering will absolutely move a production further along the process by allowing a music composition to take on its ultimate form as a documented piece of recorded sound.

In Method #5, you will learn a wide variety of recording methods from a digital recording device on your smart phone to a handheld recorder, all the way up to a multimillion dollar microphone and recording studio setup. The truth is, gone are the days where a designated audio recording engineer is needed, as we have the ability to record at audio qualities that are arguably equal to, if not better than, what is available in the top of the market. There is no dogma for recording methods, although there is always a preferred method for individuals and for the productions; you as a producer will learn to make the best decision on the best recording process for each project.

Mixing and Mastering

"Learn the rules like a pro, so you can break them like an artist."

—Pablo Picasso

Mixing and mastering is the art form of balance and soundscape. This art form is an essential piece of the music production process; it is not only the giftwrapping, but the finished gift itself.

Balance   ## Soundscape

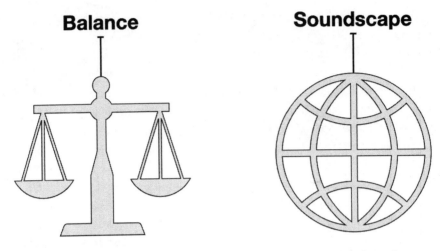

Balance   There are countless books, and formal and informal training material, on mixing and mastering. A common misconception is that music needs to be mixed in a very specific way to sound great. The truth is, if you can hear everything that needs to be heard, the mix is balanced, and consists of the bare essentials that may constitute a mixdown of music. Yet, that's like saying once tomato sauce is added to spaghetti, the dish is complete. Yes, it may taste great, but that's not where it necessarily ends, as many other ingredients can be added for additional flavor.

Let's consider balance as if we have a band on a stage: a trumpet, a pianist, a drummer, and a bassist. Imagine the band members all lined up on the stage, and they start playing. The piano is soft, and the bass is pumping a low tone throughout the groove. The drums are loud, but not overpowering, and the trumpet player takes a step to the front of the stage and plays a solo as the main focus, now the loudest on stage. This is balance: all of the members are working to not overpower each other. Nothing fancy, nothing more than controlling their sound level, listening to each other, with the trumpet stepping closer to the audience to let his lead solo shine. A mixdown of music can recreate this with various audio engineering and editing techniques to replicate what we're used to hearing in the real world, along with creating scenarios that only can be heard through the creativity of this mixdown. The mixing engineer has the choice and the artistic freedom to keep the balance as realistic to life as possible, or alternatively, to stretch the art into a new world and bring listeners in for a ride of their own.

Soundscapes   Similar to the art form of balance, the art of sound-scapes can transport a listener to any location in the world, all the way to a faraway unimaginable environment. The sound of rain can make you feel like you're outside, dripping wet and cold; the sound of crickets can bring the mood of a summer night; the sound of lava bubbling can make you feel like you are within a dangerous environment that you would rarely be in, or hear music from. The art of soundscapes is an incredible tool to understand as you can not only make creative decisions for your listeners, but essential decisions as a producer. Rather than recording in a million-dollar studio, you can use soundscapes to make a singer in a bedroom sound like they are in a cave somewhere across the world, or in a high-ceilinged church, or even replicate the sound of a famous recording studio. As you will learn in Method #6, "Mixing and Master-ing," the art of soundscapes will allow you as a producer to make not only creative decisions, but also decisions to save time, costs, and value for your productions.

APPLICATION TO YOUR PRODUCTIONS

The understanding of these various elements of music production are an essential piece of a music producer's workflow. As the process is demystified, many walls of uncertainty are removed to create a clearer path for the producer to plan a strategy while allowing space for cre-ative freedom to take place. Most importantly, students of music pro-duction must understand what needs to be adjusted if the process is not working properly. Take my student, Chase, from Method #1, whose goal was to release his first EP. Chase was able to achieve his goal, and was able to do it by improving his skills in specific areas along with bringing on team members to support other elements of the process. To understand what these areas were, Chase first needed to under-stand these three things:

1. How he was writing his music
2. How he was sound designing and recording his music
3. How he was mixing and mastering his music

If he understands how each of these elements are being achieved, then he can evaluate and reflect on what needs to be improved. If he finds areas where an element is not only lacking in quality, but ignored completely, that is an opportunity to improve the process as well.

From my perspective, I could see where Chase had a natural talent for some elements of the process, but lacked skill in others. I was able to see where he could easily grow, and where he needed to take time to develop other elements, leading to outsourcing parts of the process team members. My ability to see this was not solely because I was viewing Chase from an outside perspective, but because I knew what to look for.

At first Chase could not understand where to find these things. He told me he didn't write music; he told me that he didn't sound design, or even record his music. He told me that he did some sound design and mixing, and that's about it. I then explained stories from working with multiple bands and artists, going through my experiences with the entire production process: how we wrote songs, how we designed the sound of them, and how we mixed them. I shared how each element of the process is showcased in ways that were different from other productions.

Chase ended up seeing a clear opening in his own music production workflow, along with revealing how much more he was actually doing in his own process. He learned that the way he organized samples and MIDI loops on his laptop *was* song writing; he learned that the way he input MIDI notes into his music *was* recording. He learned not only the elements of a production, but the elements *he* utilizes in his own production, along with the elements *others* could help him achieve.

The reason Chase was able to hone in on what to improve and what to outsource was because he was trained to visualize the production process from a bird's-eye view, which revealed what was working and what was creating a roadblock to achieving his goals. Here's an exercise we did together, to make this happen. In the exercise shown in Method #1, Chase wrote down problems with his own production, with a solution written as a self or team desire. In this method, Chase will complete the same exercise, but extend the problem into a specific element of the music production process. This exercise is focused on:

1. Writing a goal
2. Writing a problem that created a roadblock to that goal

3. Identifying a specific element of this problem
4. Writing two possible routes to fix this problem—either on your own, or with a team.

Let me show you a few examples of solving problems within a specific element of your process through a desire to work on *your own*, or with *a team* to achieve your goal.

Goal: I want to release an EP this summer.

1. **Problem:** I can't write a catchy melody. (Element: song writing)
   a. **Self desire:** I want to get better at converting the ideas in my head to a musical composition.
   b. **Team desire:** I want to include a song writer on my team.
2. **Problem:** My lead synths sound too weak. (Element: sound design)
   a. **Self desire:** I want to develop my understanding of timbre and emotion for designing synths.
   b. **Team desire:** I want to include a sound designer on my team.
3. **Problem:** My mix doesn't sound "professional" enough. (Element: mixing)
   a. **Self desire:** I want practice and build experience with balance and soundscapes to make my mixes sound better.
   b. **Team desire:** I want to include a mixing and mastering engineer on my team.

Similar to the exercise in Method #1, you can see how these desires to solve a single problem differ with the addition of focusing on a single element in your process. Each of those statements above are conversations that many producers are having inside their own minds. If you are fortunate enough to understand your own process, you can now choose a solution to a problem with a clear understanding of why and where this fits into your own process of music production. While these are examples from my own students' experiences, when I personally wrote down the thoughts that I was having in direct relation to my goals, I did four things to try to understand and find a solution to each of these problems.

1. I wrote hundreds of phrases that I used to say to myself when I was trying to identify and solve the problems myself.
2. I categorized each problem as an element of the music production process.
3. I looked online in forums, videos, articles, and groups to see how others were solving these same problems.
4. I determined whether I, or a team member, is not only capable of solving my issues, but had a *desire* to solve them.

Exercise

> Imagination is more important than knowledge.
>
> —Albert Einstein

We haven't even scratched the surface of what you'll learn throughout this book. And that's exactly what this exercise represents: assessment and reflection. To grow as a producer, it's important to understand where you currently stand both technically and creatively. Your imagination is your strongest asset in bringing your productions to a new level, so I want you to prepare your imagination to spark creativity for when it is most needed during your production workflow. Preparing with possibilities before these are needed, will allow your creativity to run on autopilot, as these ideas will become second nature for your practice and preparation. For this reason, I want you to do this exercise no matter how little or how much experience you may have. This exercise will prepare you for what to think about when taking on a production. You will be able to do this with any experience level, as this exercise is focused solely on your creativity.

Write down at least a dozen things that you are saying or thinking as you face a problem that is creating a roadblock in a specific element of your production workflow (song writing and arranging, sound design and recording, mixing and mastering), or something you imagine could be an obstacle in the future. Then, determine if this is something *you* desire to solve on your own, or a *team member* desires to solve for you. Finally, write what this desire would be. This is something you should be doing every day. I'm always reflecting on the questions and statements that I am saying or thinking as I decide how to move forward with a production of music.

If you are new to production and do not yet understand how to solve potential problems, use your imagination to "guess" how they can be solved. Sometimes your own imagination and creativity can solve a problem through instinct and determination, thus increasing your experience through trial and error. Even if avoiding the trial-and-error process may be your reason for reading this book, in Section II, "An In-Depth Perspective on Music Production," we will cover many aspects of music production that can guide your understanding on how to solve the problems within individual elements of your production process. As you read this book, and develop as a producer over time, the more this exercise will adjust to your knowledge and experience. The more problems you face and solve will naturally increase your all-around abilities as a producer, so make a continual effort to revisit and utilize this exercise to assess your current experience level and reflect on what you need to develop to achieve your production goals.

3

UNDERSTAND YOUR ORDER

As a recording musician, there was always an order of production that was not only preferred, but *necessary*. In order to produce music, the musicians needed to: (1) write a song; (2) be good at performing the song; (3) record the song, and; (4) mix the song and make it sound good. Simply put, this is how it worked: (1) write; (2) rehearse; (3) record; (4) mix. But this wasn't the only way to do things. There were many times where we simply went into a recording session, not really knowing what we wanted to play. We would hit record, and then use the ideas we recorded to turn into a song. We rearranged, and removed a piece from the order: (1) record; (2) write; (3) mix. One thing I learned through this is that no matter how much we rearranged the order of the process, the mixing element was always at the end of the process. This was not because we thought this was the way it *should* work; it was really the only way it *could* work. You can't mix what you don't have, and you can't really go back and write and record without mixing again; the mix was always the final step.

Now, this process is something that I couldn't have imagined to be so important to the way I would produce music from that point on. Let's move a few years down the line, when I decided to move on to producing music on my own, on my computer, with a DAW. I remember studying audio recording at college, and spending all of my additional time in the school cafeteria playing with Ableton Live, a DAW that looked and felt like nothing I had ever seen before in music creation. This was software on my computer that allowed me to not only multitrack record audio and MIDI onto unlimited tracks, but also sound design, mix, master, and perform live, all at the same time, with a single device. It was absolutely amazing, mind-blowing, and extremely fun. I remember how quickly I dove into chopping up audio samples, adding my own synth parts, adjusting the mixdown, recording new vocal snippets in, adding audio effect, and having the time of my life. I then realized that I wasn't really going anywhere with these ideas. Yes, I was having fun, and yes, I was being creative, but I quickly saw myself going down a path of simply creating all of these interesting ideas with no end. I had no goal—I was simply creating because I enjoyed doing so. Now, if this is what you want to do, then great, definitely continue doing so. However, I wanted to complete what I started, and I needed to take a step back and reflect on what was going on. I needed to understand why I had the most powerful music-making tool in the world at my fingertips, yet I couldn't create anything that I considered "complete." I then remembered the process I went through with all of the bands I played with—the song writing, sound designing, recording, mixing, the mastering process. I didn't associate that process with the tool I had in front of me, and I can say now that once I did, I immediately changed the way I was not only creating music, but completing it.

I started reorganizing my mindset; I would distinguish the song writing stage from the sound design stage, while maintaining creative freedom within each stage, until the song was ready to move forward with a mixdown. I may have touched the faders to balance things here and there, but nothing too detailed, just enough to keep things sounding balanced while maintaining the momentum of the project. I would move forward with the process on my own as if I handing my computer to a new person in the process, although it was me alone taking on these different roles in the production process. This was the moment when everything clicked, and I was producing and completing musical projects not only by myself on my laptop, but also with the involvement of team members for later projects.

PRINCIPLES

You now understand what constitutes music production. Like any other production of material, there must be a process and order to make this happen. So, what is the best way to move forward with this? Is there a best way? The truth is, there is no single process for moving forward with your productions, although there are definitely more efficient ways to do so. This will be different for everyone, and that's where understanding your own personal workflow will assist your order.

Your Plan of Action

There are infinite ways to proceed with a production of music, but here are the two most common paths to achieve results through a proven system.

1. Song writing and arranging → sound design and recording → mixing and mastering
2. Sound design and recording → song writing and arranging → mixing and mastering

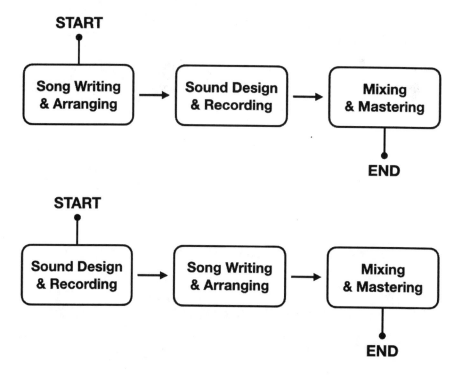

Let's discuss these two paths. The first is a common path for music producers who are confident starting a production with the music composition of a song—a skeleton, let's say. Once the composition is ready, the instrumentation, or *sound design* may be applied. From there the balancing, or *mixing*, can tie the whole production together. In an ideal world, this is the most efficient process, as the room for trial and error is minimized after the music composition is settled in.

The second is a common path for the experimentalist, the person who is inspired by sounds, textures, and feeling over musical composition. This person more commonly will be inspired to write a composition based on the sounds he or she is creating, the instruments selected, or the recordings that person is listening to.

In the end, either of these paths may be faster, or more efficient, or better overall, depending on the person. A certain path may open up instantly for one person, and take hours or weeks for another; the thing is to find the path that works best for yourself and for the team you are working with to produce music. At the end of this method, we'll move forward with an exercise to help you decide the best path for your own productions.

Diverging from the Plan

Here's a real-life lesson for you: things don't always go the way you plan. No matter how much time you put into writing your song, no matter how carefully you thought out the sound of your synthesizer parts, no matter how much you loved the idea you heard a moment ago, you never know when a new, great idea will suddenly appear. Of course it's best in most cases to move forward, but sometimes these moments are too good to pass up, and they are *essential* to add to the project even though they didn't exist moments ago. This is one of the most difficult aspects of being producer—understanding how important it is to add something, even though this something is disrupting the flow of the plan.

Now, there's a common reason for this unexpected inspiration. Unexpected inspiration is like a gift from the gods, an idea that comes out of nowhere and is absolutely *perfect*. As great as this sounds, there are some cons to this as well. Let's jump into some pros and cons of unexpected inspiration and how it can divert you from your original plan if not controlled.

The Pros and Cons of Unexpected Inspiration **The pros:** As shown in table 3.1, you can see that unexpected inspiration may increase the likability of your music, along with providing relief as a creator. The reason for this is pretty simple and has been tested over time by hit song creators explaining how their "brilliant idea" simply came to them unexpectedly. More often than not, when an idea comes out of nowhere and you can't seem to get it of your head, that same idea will trigger others. The reason for this is not fully understood as cases vary with each scenario, but a realistic example might be when you're in the shower and you sing a little melody that you really love, or you're washing the dishes and you start whistling a melody that you absolutely love at that very moment. It's very likely that someone else will like it too, and if you're able to hone these unexpected ideas into something for your productions, it is very likely that others will become increasingly interested in your productions as well, reasons they can't even explain.

Table 3.1. Pros and Cons of Unexpected Inspiration

Pros	Cons
Increase in *likability*	Disruption of *plans*
Increase in *relief*	Uncertainty of *time*

Another great thing about unexpected inspiration is that it's absolutely relieving. Very commonly, whether you thought about a musical idea for five minutes or five weeks, the moment a great idea hits it brings relief as this allows you to move forward to the next step of the process. As for making the most from your experiences, here's a tip to double down on the pros of unexpected inspiration. There are moments when you may sing, hum, or play a musical idea that other people—friends, acquaintances, or even strangers—react to instantly. Take notice of these moments, whether it is someone else repeating what you have just played, them moving their body or nodding their heads, or asking you what you just played, or any type of reaction to a spontaneous idea is worth taking note of, as these ideas may be enjoyed by a larger group of people.

The cons: As unexpected inspiration has a list of pros, there are definitely some drawbacks to this as well, and these can gradually lead to disruptions to your plans, and result in time uncertainties. These cons are not restricted to music production, but all forms of creative output across a wide range of trades. Take an artist, for example, who is painting a portrait of a woman sitting on the grass in an open field. The artist has already chosen the canvas, sketched out the woman, and applied paint to the portrait. The paint has dried and the artist has achieved a near-completed work, with a plan to deliver the painting to the art gallery first thing the next morning.

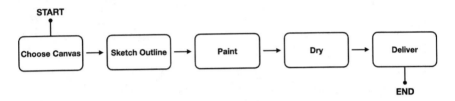

However, while looking at this nearly completed portrait, this artist imagined how great it would look if there were some trees in the background, how great it would be if there were some elements in the foreground like plants and flowers, how the tone of the sky could showcase more emotion with adjustment into a sunset rather than a blue mid-day sky. The artist believes that these changes would absolutely make the art *better*. This unexpected inspiration to add one or all of these elements will definitely disrupt the plan and may possibly delay the delivery date of this painting to the art gallery, although it is a choice that the artist needs to make—to accept or ignore these impulsive creative choices outside of the intended plan.

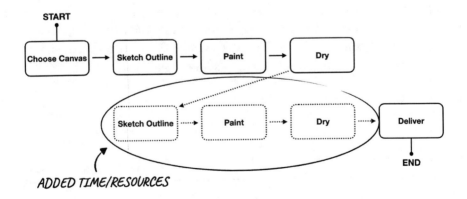

ADDED TIME/RESOURCES

This is one of the most common and difficult decisions to make as a creator, as these moment often appear when viewing a work in progress, or even near the end of a completed work. The reason for this is not fully known, although it's not uncommon to imagine additional elements for a nearly completed project and be inspired to create more based on the elements you currently see in front of you, even when someone else may view the work as "complete." You may already be relating to this in some form, and may have encountered this situation in the past as well. As a music producer, this can come in the shape or form of a song composition idea, a timbre or emotion from an instrument, all the way to the balance of a single instrument in the final mixdown. This leads to uncertainty regarding time, as you as a creator may always have *more* to add to make the project "perfect."

The great thing about this con is that although it's not *always* possible to contain this creative workflow, it is definitely possible to direct this creativity into a specific part of your workflow when needed. Here are a few ways to accomplish this.

- Decide on a goal and stick to it. If our artist from the example above knew from the beginning that he or she would paint a scene with a sunset, this wouldn't need to be altered later on. And if the artist decided on a goal unrelated to the sunset and simply wanted to showcase a woman enjoying her time in an open field, then this sunset nor added trees would not have much (or any) impact on the final work of art. As a music producer, the better you can define your goals, the more you can avoid additional and possibly even "useless" or "destructive" elements to your works of art.
- Work within a deadline. This is a common solution to knowing when to complete a project, as you literally have no opportunity to continue with the project. Creating hard deadlines that must be met will immensely improve your workflow and completion rate. Studies of creativity often show that we are most creative just moments before a deadline occurs. Working up until the final moments of a deadline is not always the best option, though it is definitely better in most cases to work up until that moment rather than not knowing where the finish line is.

- Trust your gut. This is incredibly difficult for a novice up to an intermediate producer, although with increased experience you will be able to learn what works and what does not through past mistakes and successes, allowing you to trust the ideas that first enter your mind. More often than not, your immediate thought or reaction may be the most honest, natural, and correct for a creative project. For example, think about something simple, like eating a food you either like or dislike. The moment you bite into it, you will immediately know whether it tastes good or bad. The more you think about it, the more you consider the ingredients, or consider what other people say about this food, could alter your liking of this food. In the end, your initial reaction to this food will often be your truest feeling, and this very commonly works in the same way with creative decisions.

Now, inspiration is not something we can always trigger on the spot. This is not only an art form of its own, but a scientific study—where does inspiration come from? For some, inspiration is everything, and some productions of music cannot be achieved without it. As a producer it is absolutely essential to understand not only how music works, but how the mind works creatively to jump-start these moments of inspiration to make the best of your chosen path. This could involve creating an experience, a mood, a setting in which to compose, all the way to choosing the right instruments and tones in a production or the best environment in which to mix and master a production. Such preparation may not only jump-start the creative process but end a music production on an inspiring note.

To tackle this con even further, Method #7: "Modern Problems and Solutions," will share insights on moving forward through creative roadblocks, and provide understanding of your "final steps" of a production along with understanding the true meaning of "perfection" and striving toward this in your own work.

Awareness of Your Plan

Here is the most real-life lesson of all: things don't always work. Let me say that again: things do not always work, and they commonly do not go according to plan; your awareness of this will allow you to align your plan to not only adapt to these changes, but anticipate them. Again, let's talk about inspiration. The truth is that we never know when inspiration will hit, no matter how much we focus on honing in on that moment. And the truth is, that's okay. The role of a producer is not to fight with this force, but utilize it on our path and choose when it's best to be rigid in the process. For example, say we go with path 1 and write a song, record a song, and then mix the song, and everything is going as planned. Then suddenly, while the song is being mixed, inspiration hits. Everybody in the room hears a moment in the song that would sound great with a new added composition, a new vocal part. Is it wrong to add it into the song at this moment? Are we now out of order? Is this going to slow down production? Well, yes, this is going to slow things down. Although, is this bad? That's your role as a producer to decide. Is there enough time, is there the right equipment, will this make or break the production? Will this cost more money? Do we have enough money to record the new vocal part? Again, you as a producer need to make the decision to keep moving forward, or to break the process and record the new part.

In the end, there are no correct or incorrect choices. There are simply choices made to enhance the efficiency, time, cost, and delivery of a project. You may be so efficient that you have enough time left to record that extra part. That's what this book is focused on—not telling you to follow a specific path, but to create a path that is so strong and efficient that you can afford these moments when things don't work according to plan. Expect this to happen and take it into account. By doing this, you are already preparing to keep things in line and continue with your plan.

The awareness of this process will keep you on track to what you need and know when you need it. With time, experience, and practice, you'll create not only a network of individuals to work with, but a team to produce absolutely amazing music projects.

The important thing is to make progress. The most common flaw of producers, or any type of leader, is a lack of decision making and a firm belief in moving forward. If you believe something is complete, then it's time to move on. It's understanding that there will always be a next step leading closer toward perfection, but it doesn't mean this thing you're working on right now will be that step to perfection.

APPLICATION TO YOUR PRODUCTIONS

Understanding the order of your process is absolutely essential to moving forward with your productions, and this is not only applicable to a certain type of person with one type of workflow. Let's take a look at two of my students, with two very different styles of workflow, but with a common goal of completing a production of music.

Let's call these students, Chase and Elle. Chase is the student we discussed in Method #1 and Method #2, with the goal of releasing an EP. Chase was hitting a few roadblocks with his production that did not allow him to complete his songs, although when I took a look at his project files (digital files of multitrack audio and MIDI recordings), I was able to see that he was not short of ideas. He had more ideas than I could even think of at the time—over twenty projects that were actually really great, although all were brief musical ideas, with *potential* to be something great. Many people see this as a weakness, the inability to bring a musical idea to completion, and while it is true that this is definitely *not* a strength, within these great ideas there was most definitely a creative strength, and that's the point Chase and I looked for in order to move forward with his production. From there, he was able to isolate his weakness and figure out how to fill in this gap on his own or with a team, as seen in Method #1.

After a discussion with Chase, I had him explain his method of how he came up with his ideas, and it was no surprise that he followed a similar workflow for all twenty projects: he started with a "cool sound," whether that was a sample, a synth preset, or even custom designing the sound of an instrument. Then he was inspired by that "cool sound" and created a melody, chords, or even bass lines with these sounds. Simply put, he started with *sound design*, and then progressed further with *song writing and arranging*. With this, we were easily able to see that his strengths were in sound design, leading to inspiration to create melodies and other musical compositions, although his lack of music theory and song writing skills created a roadblock to moving further along with his productions. Because we could identify this challenge, we were able to hone in on how to solve this issue, and we ended up diving deep into building his knowledge, practice, and experience with song writing and arranging, leading to an immense increase in Chase's production output.

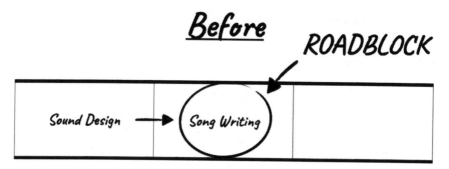

As seen in Method #1, Chase was able to achieve his goal of releasing his EP by his deadline, and this method of understanding his order was in fact an essential piece leading to his achievement.

My other student, Elle, is a piano player, singer, and song writer. She has an incredible talent for song writing, arranging, and musical performance, and the musical ideas she has presented to me were incredible songs on their own. The thing is, these songs alone were not her intended goal; rather, her goal was not to produce and perform these songs as a piano and vocal production, but to expand the sound, instrumentation, and textures of her compositions with electronic music production and instrumental recording. Unlike Chase, Elle had the strength of starting a music production project with the song writing and arranging process, but hit roadblocks when it came to sound design and recording; she didn't know how to utilize software synthesizers; she didn't know how to record MIDI into her computer and adjust the timbre of her instruments digitally; she didn't understand how to find proper virtual instruments to produce the sounds she was striving for. Throughout our discussions and lessons, we were able to find the right tools for her production needs and ended up not even needing an additional team member for her production up until the mixing and mastering phase.

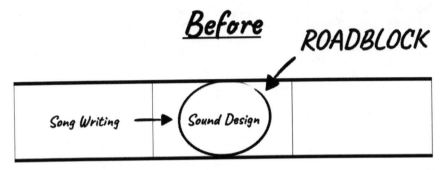

Elle was able to move forward all of her musical ideas from the song writing and arranging phase to the sound design and recording phase, to then pass the project over to a mixing and mastering engineer to finalize the balance and final touches of her music productions, achieving her goals in the end.

These two students had completely different orders for starting and progressing with their productions, although they were both able to achieve their goals by understanding and refining the order of their process. As a music producer, it's important to figure out the path that works for you or your team members involved in your productions. For example, if you bring on a team member that is incredible at sound design, and you bring on another team member that is great at composing music with inspiration from the sound of the instruments, then this pair would work well together starting with the sound design phase and then moving to the song writing phase. The strengths and weaknesses of the people involved in your production must be added together when deciding the best path on which to take your production. As you build experience with making the best of the skills that you or your team possess, you will grow as a producer, increasing your production output.

Also take into consideration that there are people who are strong in starting with either song writing/arranging and sound design/recording, and allow this person to be an essential piece of a production because he or she is capable of starting from whichever element of the process that your production needs in any given moment. It's your role as a producer to understand when and where to utilize this person most, whether it be yourself or a team member with this dual skill set.

Both of my students needed to understand their strengths as creators and producers to determine the best place to start and make progress in their productions. Here's an exercise we did together to make this happen. Whenever the students were hitting a roadblock in their production workflow, we identified all of the strengths that were present up to this point while also identifying the weaknesses that caused the roadblock. If there was a moment of strength that led to a weakness, it was better to start with their strengths in their production order to solve the weakness. If the moment of strength was inspired by their weakness, then it was better to solve the weakness in order to move forward with their strengths in the production order. This exercise incorporates concepts from previous exercises under Method #1 and Method #2. This exercise is focused on:

1. Writing your strengths as a creator
2. Writing your weaknesses as a creator
3. Writing two possible routes to fix the problem stated above, either on your own, or with a team
4. Write a potential order for your production

Let me show you a few examples of identifying your production order through assessing your strengths as a creator.

- **Strength:** I can create many song ideas by starting with a cool synth sound.

- **Weakness:** I can only create short ideas that do not turn into full song.
  - **a. Self desire:** I want to learn more about writing music.
  - **b. Team desire:** I want to include a song writer on my team.
- **Order:** Sound design and recording → song writing and arranging

- **Strength:** I can write many full songs on piano.
- **Weakness:** I don't know how to turn my song into a full electronic music production with high-quality synths and sound design.
  - **a. Self desire:** I want to learn more about synthesis and sound design.
  - **b. Team desire:** I want to include a sound designer on my team.
- **Order:** Song writing and arranging → sound design and recording

- **Strength:** I am great at sound designing synthesizers for electronic pop music.
- **Weakness:** I can't design a synth without being inspired by a melody.
  - **a. Self desire:** I want to learn more about song writing.
  - **b. Team desire:** I want to include a song writer on my team.
- **Order:** Song writing and arranging → sound design and recording

Do you see a pattern with these answers that lead to a clear order? Understanding your strengths and weaknesses will allow you to decide on the order for your production process that can increase efficiency in your workflow, leading to higher production output.

Each of the statements above are conversations that many producers have in their own minds. While these are examples from my own students' experience, when I wrote down my own thoughts regarding my production strengths and weaknesses, I did four things to try to find a solution to my problems.

1. I wrote hundreds of phrases that I used to say to myself when I was trying to identify and solve the problems myself.
2. I looked online in forums, videos, articles, groups, and with mentors to see how others were solving these same problems.

3. I determined whether I, or a team member, is not only capable of solving my issues, but *desires* to solve them.
4. I determined the most efficient order that allows my strengths to make progress throughout the production process.

Exercise

For this exercise, write down at least a dozen things that you are saying or thinking as you're observing your creative output in your production workflow. Then, write down at least a dozen things that you are saying or thinking as you face a problem that is creating a roadblock in your production workflow, or something you imagine could be an obstacle in the future. Then, determine whether this is something *you* desire to solve on your own, or a *team member* desires to solve for you. Next, write down what this desire would be. Finally, write the order of elements that push your production in a healthy direction. This is something you should be doing every day. I'm always considering the questions and statements that I am saying as I decide how to move forward with a music project. As I did with the previous exercises, I'll state the truth once again: most people, myself included, cannot see what the issues are until we stop, think, and reflect on them.

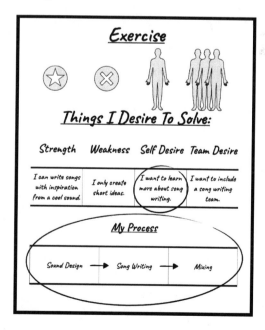

II

AN IN-DEPTH PERSPECTIVE ON MUSIC PRODUCTION

In this section you will dive into three methods that give you an in-depth perspective on music production. This is how the methods in this section are laid out:

1. Each method begins with a story, a true personal experience related to the topic and learning experiences provided.
2. This story then leads to principles to take away from these experiences.
3. This is followed by a personal experience I had with my students, where these principles were applied.
4. Each method concludes with an exercise for you to do to improve your own music production skill sets.

4

SONG WRITING AND ARRANGING

I was sitting in a cafe near Ebisu Station in Tokyo, Japan, across the table from someone I would soon call a great friend—Chanu, a Korean fashion designer with a level of talent and unmatched dedication, a true visionary of his craft. Sitting beside him was his fashion brand's director and live-events producer; the reason for this meeting was to discuss an opportunity that would change my entire outlook on music production. This meeting covered the pre-production plan for a Fashion Week runway event—specifically, Amazon Tokyo Fashion Week.

While sitting at this meeting, I wondered how and why I had arrived here, invited to "create the music for a runway show," as at the time I had no idea what this would entail; my idea of a fashion show was models walking down a runway with a DJ playing chic techno tracks to the beat of their steps. I couldn't have been more wrong. I learned at this meeting and throughout the next four weeks leading up to the event what exactly this project would entail, and it led to a deep appreciation for not only the world of fashion, but the involvement of music in this industry. I also learned about the high level of production required from all aspects of the production team, which strongly influences the way I produce music today. For this event, my role as a music producer was to create an original soundtrack spanning twenty minutes for a runway show, and this music was to be performed in real time, with sound cues for the models, lighting team, and various production units so that a smooth show outline was followed. Simply put, I would create music that provides an emotional impact for the audience while at the same time secretly informing the models and lighting team what to do, based on my song form and sound cues. It was something I had never done before, nor even knew existed, and I was incredibly excited to be a part of this event.

The song writing process for this event was unlike anything I had done previously. I came from a background of performing with musicians, bands, and song writers who would either present "skeletons" of songs as a basic outline, and the rest of the band would add their ideas, or else we would sit together and create something from scratch based on what felt right. I'm incredibly grateful to have experienced those song writing moments, as they shaped the music creator I am today. But this event was completely different. I was introduced to clothing lines, accessories, fabrics, metals, and story lines for the event; told what the pieces of clothing meant and what message the fashion line portrayed; these became my references for how the music was to be emotionally driven and how it would tell Chanu's story as a fashion designer.

Chanu's brand, which connects cultures, time periods, and streetwear, led to a combination of hard trap music influenced by industrial and ethnic percussive elements, This resulted in a production of music in a genre I have never stepped into before. The Fashion Week work pushed my own boundaries as a musician who previously played drums in rock, pop, and jazz groups. I produced hard trap and hip-hop music for an event broadcast to millions of people via television and online media sources, and even throughout the city of Tokyo as I (accidentally) caught the event, along with my soundtrack, playing on an LED billboard near the world's largest city crosswalk in Shibuya, Tokyo.

From that first meeting to the day of the event, we only had four weeks. But we had a goal, we had a deadline, and we had a creative vision for this project. As a music producer, I had to make choices to bring these ideas to life, and this all started with the song writing element of the production. I needed to figure out what worked for this genre of music, I needed to experiment with sounds I had never worked with, I needed to use tools I had never used to achieve the sound I was striving for, and most importantly, I needed to trust my ideas, as I was the sole person involved in this production. I was producing this music on my own, and I needed to make choices that would push my production further along, avoiding or solving as many roadblocks as I could throughout each step of the process.

The show was a success, and led to an additional eight seasons of Fashion Week runway events with Chanu and his brand, where we built a bond and creative trust to push each production further as we progressed through each event as a creative team.

PRINCIPLES

It's hard for most of us to remember, but it actually wasn't that long ago that we created music very differently from how we do it today. There were very few (or even no way) to create music on mobile devices, computers, or electronic sequencers. There were recording studios, rehearsal spaces, and a need for musical instruments (and people to play them) to allow music creators to share their thoughts and ideas for a song.

The process of "writing a song" is continuously adjusting with developments in technology, and it's important for a music producer to be up-to-date on the options available. In this method, we will discuss four common ways to write and arrange music, along with explaining how to choose the best team member or individual to work with, if you want to oversee this process on your own.

Getting Involved with Song Writing and Arranging

In Method #2, you learned about song writing and arranging from a bird's-eye view; in this method, we'll break down common roles for song writing and arranging, along with common practices when writing and arranging your own music. Let's start off with the roles.

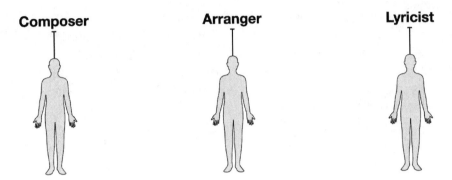

Composer   **Arranger**   **Lyricist**

Three common roles involved with the song writing and arranging process of a music production are (1) music composer, (2) music arranger, and (3) lyricist. You may have heard these titles before, and if you haven't, here is a quick breakdown if you are looking for someone to fill one of these roles for your own production.

Music Composer: A music composer creates an original piece of music. The role of a music composer can lead the process of writing melody, harmony, rhythm, and dynamic movement for a song. Simply put, this is the person who writes the story of your entire song.

Music Arranger: A music arranger is often mistaken for a music composer, and here is the big difference: a music arrangement is an *adaptation* of a composition for a new purpose. This means that the arranger can take an original music composition and rewrite, or *rearrange* the composition for a new instrument, group of instruments, or performance scenario. Simply put, a music arranger will create a new version of a music composition.

Lyricist: Not all songs have singers and lyrics, although when they do, the lyricist handles this. This role is historically known as a poet or writer, but in the context of music, a lyricist. The lyrics are often sung or spoken by a group or individual singer.

These are three common roles, and there is no rule that these roles must be divided among three individuals. It is very common that a music composer is both an instrumentalist and a singer, a song writer and a song arranger, or a combination of the three. In the end, it's not solely about finding a person who is capable of handling these roles, but how well they perform them.

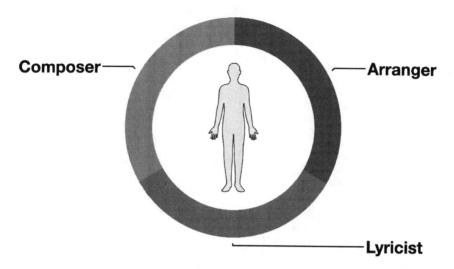

For example, a common goal for an arranger is to rearrange a song that was originally intended for a single instrument to a song for a group of instruments, such as a full orchestra. In this case, a music arranger with an orchestral composition or arranging background may be a great fit for this role; it's all about choosing a person who can push your production forward in the right direction.

Producer Takeaway: If you are not handling the song writing and arranging portion on your own, you will most likely be reaching out to somebody with some or all of these talents. It's up to you to determine your production needs, and find the person that will move your production forward in the best way possible.

You now understand who will handle these roles; let's now discuss four common ways they will do this, along with some prerequisites for doing so. The prerequisites are explained for two reasons: (1) If you want to find somebody to do it, you'll know what to look for, and (2) if you want to do it yourself, you'll know what you need to do it.

Musical Notation Let's start off with the most formal approach to writing and arranging music. And I mean this in the most literal form—actually writing the music by hand. When it comes to any spoken language, there is a written counterpart to communicate the language on paper, and it is the same for music. Musical notation is the written language of music, and this written language is a representation of individual pitches, rhythms, and dynamics of the sound spectrum as humans know it. Let me explain where this comes from, and why it may be important for your productions.

We first need to understand what this written language is communicating: sound. Simply put, there is a spectrum of sound that we can hear; humans are capable of hearing from 20Hz up to 20kHz (dogs can hear up to 45kHz, which is why they can hear high-pitched sounds that humans cannot).

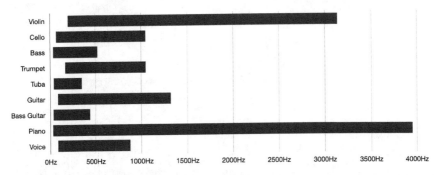

Humans have been writing music since as early as 1400 BCE. By writing, I mean carving into rock because paper wasn't yet invented. Yes, musical notation was invented before paper—that's how long it's been around. And we're still using it today, so it's relevant enough to find its way into this book.

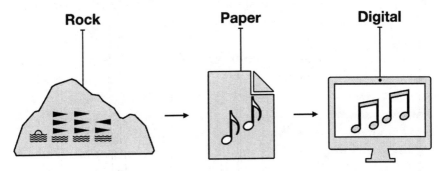

Throughout the years, musical notation has evolved to today's written language communicated through paper and digital applications. This updated form of musical notation communicates sound with incredible detail, including pitch, rhythm, dynamics, and even the emotion of a musical composition.

Producer Takeaway: If you are in need of a team member to not only conceptualize the idea for a song, but communicate these ideas to others, such as an instrumentalist, conductor, director, or anyone else who must read the music composition, then a song writer with the ability to read and write musical notation is a great addition to the production team. Let's jump into some prerequisites, pros, and cons for writing musical notation.

- Prerequisites:
  * Musical notation comprehension: one to two years of study is recommended for quality results
  * Music theory: Advanced understanding is desired, although a basic level of theory is sufficient
- Pros:
  * System easily communicates musical ideas
  * Widely known language of music
  * No instrument needed to write or arrange with musical notation
  * Easily written by hand or digitally
- Cons:
  * Takes time to learn
  * Although it is widely known, not everybody can read music
  * Requires an instrument or software to hear what's written
  * Writing music does not make you "better" at creating music; this is simply a system to communicate musical ideas

Musical Instrument   An incredibly useful way to communicate musical ideas is through a musical instrument. Whether a piano, a guitar, a ukulele, a trumpet, or anything else, the more proficient a song writer is with his or her instrument, the better that writer can communicate his or her own musical ideas. There is no generally accepted dogma for song writing and arranging instruments, as each instrument has an opportunity to inspire musical creation. However, to use a single instrument for context; I'll choose one that works very well for both acoustic and digital musical performance, song writing, and arranging, and may even take the cake for best musical design layout as well: the piano.

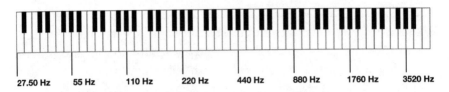

27.50 Hz   55 Hz   110 Hz   220 Hz   440 Hz   880 Hz   1760 Hz   3520 Hz

Why do I say the piano has a great musical design layout? Well, re-member how the sound spectrum is divided into musical notes. The piano allocates these same notes across each key on the piano, horizon-tally; there really couldn't be a simpler representation of musical notes on an instrument. Let's not dive too deeply into the piano here, though, because music writing can be done with any instrument.

Producer Takeaway: If your production does not require the use of written musical notation to communicate or document ideas, then utiliz-ing an instrument is a great way to naturally generate musical ideas. If you do not play any instruments, then you can bring in a team member with an instrumental performance background to help translate your ideas into musical output. Another possibility is playing around with an instrument on your own, one that you may have not even seen before, no matter your skill level. You never know what will come out if you never try. Let's jump into some prerequisites, pros, and cons for writing with a musical instrument.

- Prerequisites:
  - Musical instrument training: five to ten years is recommended for quality results
  - Music theory: Basic to advanced understanding is desired, although not required
- Pros:
  - Easily communicate musical ideas through performance
  - No need for musical notation
  - Great idea generator based on sound and feel
- Cons:
  - Years of practice is required for quality results
  - Some instruments are unattainable for various reasons (cost, noise, size, etc.)

* Some instruments are limited to a specific range of notes
* Performing on an instrument does not make you "better" at writing music; an instrument is simply a tool to communicate musical ideas
* Without musical notation or a recording device, you must memorize everything you create

MIDI and Sequencers   No matter the musical genre, the digital advancements of musical technology have led to a point where digital and acoustic sounds are almost indistinguishable; the advancement of MIDI definitely contributed to this. MIDI has become not only an industry standard, but an incredibly useful approach to writing and arranging music in genres from classical and jazz arrangements all the way to electronic music. MIDI and sequencer advancements can fully support the workflow of a song writer or arranger. As discussed previously regarding musical notation and musical instruments, MIDI and sequencers combine the best of these worlds into digital form, so let me explain why and how these can assist with your song writing and arranging workflow.

Let's start with a quick introduction to MIDI. MIDI stands for musical instrument digital interface, which is a digital language that allows computers to talk to each other. MIDI is capable of telling a computer to do anything from performing and recording a musical note, all the way to composing and arranging a full orchestral masterpiece. So, how does it do this? It's actually very simple, so I'll explain how MIDI works, how you can use it to compose and arrange music, and how this all ties into using a sequencer.

MIDI allows you to play any sound of any instrument with the use of a digital controller or electronic instrument. You can play an electronic keyboard that looks like a piano, but sounds like a saxophone, a trumpet, a full choir, or even a pack of lions roaring. These sounds are triggered by something called MIDI notes. These notes are sent out of your MIDI controller and into your computer (or sound module), which then triggers the sound.

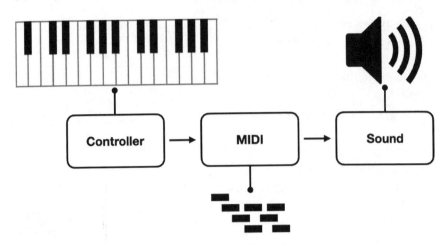

MIDI notes are not only triggered through live performance of a MIDI controller, but through two common approaches as well. The first way is through a sequencer.

There are many sequencers available, ever since the early 1980s when their popularity greatly increased. These sequencers are electronic instruments that allow a person to choose specific notes, rhythms, and dynamics to add into a looped sequence to create music. This type of song writing has led to the rise of countless musical genres, including techno, hip hop, and many more throughout the world.

The other common and most advanced way to sequence music is through a DAW (digital audio workstation).

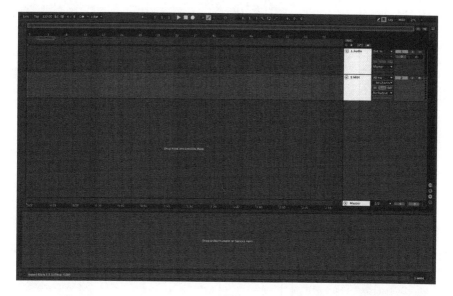

A DAW is essentially a multitrack audio recording and editing software run on laptop and desktop computers. This kind of software is extremely useful for not only recording instruments, but writing and recording MIDI as well—all the way from small loops to full song compositions and arrangements, with an incredible amount of automation to work with.

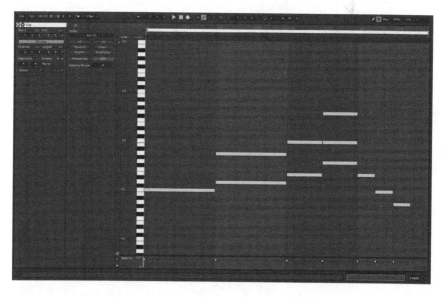

Most DAWs include a MIDI editor in a grid-like pattern that allows you to draw in and record MIDI notes, along with editing and rearranging the notes, and changing the speed of each note.

Producer Takeaway: If you are a producer requiring a wide range of instruments for your production and you do not have the means to obtain these resources, then bringing in a MIDI or somebody who knows how to handle it is definitely a useful piece of your process. Let's jump into some prerequisites, pros, and cons for writing with MIDI and a sequencer.

- Prerequisites:
  * DAW and/or electronic sequencer experience: two to five years is recommended for quality results
  * Music theory: Basic to advanced understanding is desired, although not required
- Pros:
  * Easy to create music
  * Little to no music theory needed
  * MIDI and DAWs have become an industry standard, so it's easy to share and collaborate on projects
  * Very likely to be on a portable device to create from anywhere
- Cons:
  * Stuck with digital instruments
  * Limited to what the technology can do
  * Some sequencers are limited in rhythmic range
  * Some instruments are unattainable for various reasons (e.g., cost)

Sample-Based Music   Now that you have an understanding of musical notation and MIDI, let's talk about *sample-based music*. Sample-based music is an extremely common way of creating music, especially for electronic music producers and beat makers. Sample-based music composition is focused on writing music, not only with individual pitches and chords, but *any* sound. This is known as sampling, which is the reuse of a portion (or sample) of an audio recording.

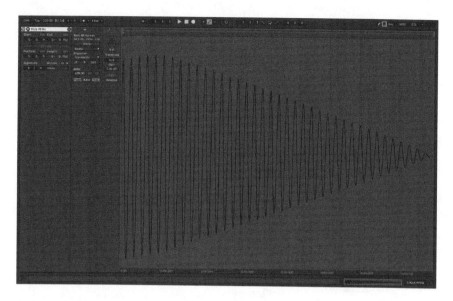

Samples may contain anything from a rhythm to a melody or chord, a person speaking, an animal growling, all the way to an entire phrase of music. Audio samples are commonly utilized with instruments called samplers. And, remember the DAW we talked about? Samplers are commonly used within these as well.

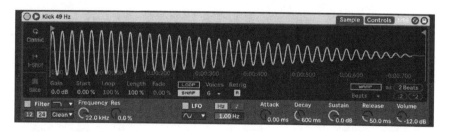

This form of musical creation emerged in the 1980s as a foundation for hip-hop music, with producers sampling funk and soul records. Drum breaks in particular would be sampled from the music, and rappers would rap over the beats. This art form has developed to where we are today and utilized in almost every music genre.

Producer Takeaway: If you are in need of musical inspiration for your production, audio samples are incredible sources of not only compositional inspiration, but tonal inspiration. There are two main types of samples to utilize: one-shot samples, and loops. One-shot samples are usually short hits like a snare drum, kick drum, or synth stab. Loops are usually samples that can be repeated over and over again and loop around to the beginning, such as a drum groove, a chord progression, or a melody. Audio samples can be found from any recorded audio in the world, although there are companies and services that offer royalty-free samples specifically made for music producers. If you are in need of a new set of sound textures and musical phrases for your production, audio samples may be the way to go. Let's jump into some prerequisites, pros, and cons for writing with samples.

- Prerequisites:
  * DAW and/or electronic sampler experience: two to five years is recommended for quality results
  * Music theory: Basic to advanced understanding is desired, although not required
- Pros:
  * Start with a good sound
  * Easy to write with
  * Easy to find great samples, with libraries available
  * The sound of sampling is widely known and accepted (at some level)
- Cons:
  * Difficulty with copyright claims
  * Difficult to know the notes and keys of a sample
  * Different to mesh samples without music theory knowledge or natural ear
  * Takes time to master the editing process of sampling

APPLICATION TO YOUR PRODUCTIONS

I remember a specific student of mine asking advice regarding a reference of my own music, specifically one that the student heard in a Fashion Week runway show. The music for this event was about twenty minutes in length, including a show introduction, main theme, breaks, sound cues, and an outro to the event. This student's reason for this reference was to explain that he felt very confident in many aspects of his production process, except for the song writing and arranging phase; specifically, composing a long form musical piece that not only tells a story but maintains movement, excitement, and doesn't sound "boring." After experiencing the twenty-minute runway event with my sample-based hard trap music playing throughout, the student wondered how I was able to expand a single musical composition into a time frame of that length, which is about the span of a full EP of music (three to five songs). This student was not alone in wondering about this; a large number of music creators struggle with the song writing and arranging element of a production.

This student had a talent for creating great song ideas with sample-based music, on his own in his bedroom, though he faced roadblocks when it came to extending these sixteen-bar "beats" into full musical compositions. I knew exactly where he was coming from, because I was once in the same place. I explained that at one time I too didn't know exactly how to expand my musical ideas, how to maintain momentum, and how to tell a story through a long-form music composition. I explained how I too made the choice to work *on my own* with this specific production, even though I had flaws as a song writer. I then explained how I overcame my weaknesses by utilizing tools such as samplers, MIDI effects, and sequencers to shape and "correct" my musical composition. I described how I divided my composition into short "chapters" with individual "themes" that were connected together with musical transitions to simplify writing a few small ideas instead of one long one. The more I explained and unveiled my own process, the more my student was able to grasp ideas to include in his own song writing and arranging process.

Following our conversation with a week of practice, this student presented two project files to me; one was a *before* and the other was an *after*. I opened the *after* first, and I saw a full song arranged from start to finish. I saw a project file with an intro, a verse, a build, a drop, another verse, a build, a drop, a break, a build, a drop, and an outro. I was viewing and listening to an entire song form arrangement that sounded far from a sixteen-bar "beat." Out of curiosity, I went back and opened up the *before* project, and this is where the student's progress was unveiled in all its glory. This project was a complete mess—a mess of creativity at its finest. There were audio samples all over the place, there were effects left and right, and there were beats on top of beats within a single project. Honestly, the beats were fine, but that's all they were. They were beats locked away as "ideas" within a project on a computer, leading to what the student learned to achieve: he learned to produce music to share with the world, as opposed to hoarding files of ideas on a hard drive, ideas that may never see the light of day.

After a detailed look into the student's project, I was able to see that he decided to utilize an approach similar to my own for creating music based on samples. To get to this point, he went through a few exercises and practice sessions to achieve these results. Here's an exercise we did together to make this happen: similar to the exercise shown in Method #1, the student was to pin down the moment in the song writing and arranging process where a roadblock was occurring, and choose whether to improve his own techniques, involve someone else to handle this role, or add a digital device to support the process. This exercise is focused on:

1. Writing a goal
2. Writing a problem in the song writing and arranging process that created a roadblock to that goal
3. Writing three possible routes to fix this problem, either on your own, with a team, or with a digital device
4. Writing the name(s) of the person or device(s) that will handle this role.

Let me show you a few examples of solving song writing and arranging problems on your own, with a team, or with digital devices. The more specific you can be with your problem, the better you can find a solution. For example, instead of stating a problem as "I don't know anything about music theory," dig deeper into something like "I don't know how to create arpeggios."

Goal: Complete a full song.

1. **Problem:** I don't know how to create arpeggios that play in the background of my song.
   a. **Self desire:** I want to learn more about music theory and harmony.
   b. **Team desire:** I want to include a song writer on my team.

  c. **Device desire:** I want to use an arpeggiator and MIDI scale device.

2. **Problem:** I don't know how to extend the form of my song.

  a. **Self desire:** I want to divide each part of my song into "chapters" and focus on writing small segments that connect together.

  b. **Team desire:** I want to include a song writer or arranger on my team.

  c. **Device desire:** I want to use a sequencer to create a song form.

Similar to Method #1, you can see how these desires regarding a single problem differ, with the addition a new team member in the form of a *device*. As a music producer, it's incredibly helpful to understand that your team members can come in the form of not only people, but electronic devices as well, such as a sampler, sequencer, or MIDI effect.

Each of those statements above are conversations that many producers have in their own minds. While these are examples from my own student's experience, when I actually wrote down the thoughts that I was having in direct relation to my own song writing and arranging process, I did four things to try to understand and find a solution to each of these problems:

1. I wrote hundreds of phrases that I used to say to myself when I was trying to solve the problems myself.
2. I looked online in forums, videos, articles, groups, and with mentors to see how others were solving these same problems.
3. I determined whether I, a team member, or a device is not only capable of solving my issues, but either *desires* or is *designed* to solve them.
4. I decided who (or what) will handle this role.

Exercise

When it comes to working with both people and devices, the opportunities to include multiple approaches to a process open up. For example, if you want to write the music to your composition on your own, you can also include a sampler or sequencer to help you out. If you want to work with a team member to write harmony and chords for your composition, you may also include the support of MIDI effects to keep your song in key. In the end, you don't need to choose to work solely on your own, or with a team; you also have the option to include a device as another "team member" in addition to either of these choices.

For this exercise, write down at least a dozen things that you are saying or thinking as you face an issue that is creating a roadblock in your song writing and arranging process, or something you imagine may become an obstacle in the future. Then, determine whether this is something *you* desire to solve on your own, a *team member* desires to solve for you, or can be solved with a device. Then, write what this desire would be. And finally, write who (or what) will handle this role. This is something you should be doing every day. I'm always aware of the questions and statements that I am saying or thinking as I decide how to move forward with a music production project. The truth is that the more experience we have as creators, the more these exercises will present themselves in a new light as we revisit them with our updated workflows and knowledge. Most people don't see what the issues are until we stop, think, and reflect on them.

5

SOUND DESIGN AND RECORDING

There were two points in my life when I completely changed my outlook on sound design. The first was when I was playing drums with a band; the next occurred a few years later, when I was producing electronic music.

I was in a recording studio, getting ready to record drum parts for a studio recording that would find its way to multiple television placements with a recording engineer I highly respected. With this all in mind, I put great effort into making my drums sound at their absolute peak of sound quality. I had a really good feel for tuning my drums; I put hours, weeks, even months (later even years) into the art of drum tuning alone, and my drums sounded really good. Once my drums were all set up and ready to record, I remember the recording engineer walking up to the kit before placing the microphones on each tom and banging the tom with a stick. He didn't even say anything, he simply walked over to a roll of paper towels, grabbed some duct tape, and started duct taping paper towels to my drum heads. Because I respected this engineer so highly, I didn't say anything at the time—I simply watched him as he was tapping my drums with his fingers and placing duct tape and paper towels in very particular locations around the edges of the drum heads. He then told me to play them again. I banged on the drum, and to my surprise, they sounded incredible; even better than before. They still had the pitch and tone I tuned in there, although they sounded tightened up and clean; they sounded "perfect." This really brought home to me how someone who doesn't even play the instrument can make it sound great through their own experience of recording that instrument. In my eyes, this was true sound design.

A few years later, I was part of another scenario, and was even more surprised by the outcome because this scenario involved some of the most popular music in the world. At this time, I was already deeply immersed in electronic music production and synth sound design. I would often sit at my computer sculpting kick drums, bass one-shots, and other sounds that were somewhat useless for a song that meant the world to me at the time. And I remember the day this all changed: when I heard the song "Epic" by Sandro Silva and Quintino. This song has a very distinctive lead pluck sound in the drop. I spent hours trying to recreate this sound. I got close, but it was never quite there, and that became my goal at the time—to recreate this sound to the dot. It got to a point where I needed to do some research to find information that could help me nail this sound, and that's when I found it. Someone posted online, in some forum, that "the one-shot sample used in the melody of *Epic by Sandro Silva & Quintino; VEC1 Sounds 074E from the Vengeance Essential Club sounds vol. 1 sample CD.*" I immediately searched for the sound, downloaded it, and to my mind-blowing surprise, this was the exact sound used in the song. This sample was used in a sampler, and pitched to play the melody. This day absolutely changed the way I thought about sound design; the simplicity of this hit song using a sample or "preset" was something I couldn't imagine being possible. And I kept seeing this appear as a trend; even while writing this book, a similar thing happened. I was listening to the number-one Billboard dance song in 2020, SAINt JHN's "Roses (Imanbek Remix)," and I loved the sound of the bass. I wanted to re-create the sound and did some research before I dove in. And once again, here was the information online: "*Vengeance EDM Essentials Vol. 2* and the sample name was *VEDM2 Bass 005 (F).*" This song's bass line was using a sample from the same exact sample company as the song that blew my mind ten years earlier. It wasn't solely a fluke; hit songs don't need to have complex sound design. The only difference was my reaction to the more recent finding, as there was no surprise factor involved. I had accepted that it's not about how the sound was made, but how it sounds in the end, and it sounded great enough to become a number-one Billboard hit.

PRINCIPLES

It wasn't that long ago when the concept of sound design focused on the type of instrument a musician was playing, the way it was tuned, or even the way it was amplified. Keeping these ideas in mind while moving forward into the world of music creation on mobile devices, computers, or electronic sequencers is an incredible skill set to have, as it opens each musical scenario to new paths of sound. The process of "sound design" is continually adjusting to developments in technology, and it's important for music producers to be up-to-date with the options available, along with understanding how this art form came about. In this method, we'll discuss four common ways to sound design and record music, along with understanding how to choose the best team member or individual to work with if you want to oversee this process alone.

Getting Involved with Sound Design and Recording

In Method #2, you learned about sound design and recording from a bird's-eye view; in this method, we'll break down common roles for sound designing and recording, along with common practices to sound design and record your own music. Let's start with the roles.

Sound Designer

Recording Engineer

Two common roles involved with the sound design and recording process of a music production are sound designer and recording engineer. You may have heard these titles before, but if you haven't, here is a quick breakdown if you're looking for someone to fill this role for your own production.

Sound Designer: The role of a sound designer is to sculpt sonic textures that the listener will hear. The role can produce the sound effects, atmosphere, sonic textures, and spatial ambience that create both natural and abstract worlds for the listener. A great sound designer understands and can utilize a wide variety of audio production tools, instruments, and psychoacoustics. Above all, and most importantly, a good sound designer has a strong developed sense of hearing and sensitivity to balance, timbre, rhythm, melody, harmony, and overall musical structure of a music production. He or she can design the sound of a group or individual instrument, sound effect, or track in a song with a strong understanding of sound and how to tell the musical story both emotionally and acoustically for the listener.

Recording Engineer: The role of a recording engineer is to document and *record* audio or MIDI. This role typically revolves around recording a live performance of musical instruments or sounds through microphones or electronic devices. The recording engineer is most commonly known for handling the "technical aspect of the recording," which involves placing microphones, setting levels, and balancing the overall sound sources being documented with the use of recording and mixing tools. Simply put, the recording engineer will be documenting all of the sound for a production of music.

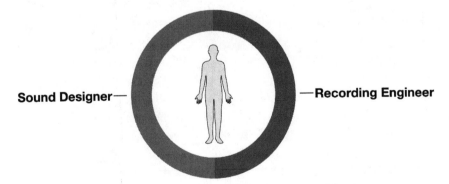

As seen in Method #4, these roles do not need to be divided between two different people. It is very common for a sound designer to be a musical instrumentalist, a song writer, or even a recording engineer as well. On the other end of the spectrum, there are some recording engineers who focus on very specific tasks such as only setting up microphones, manipulating the tone of synthesizers, or anything in between. In the end, there is no set-in-stone approach to bringing a sound designer or recording engineer to your production; it's mainly about your time and available resources as a producer to decide on how many people to bring into the production and how well each person performs his or her role.

Producer Takeaway: If you are not handling the sound design and recording process on your own, you will most likely be reaching out to someone having some or all of these talents. It's up to you to figure out your production needs and find the person that will push your production forward in the best way possible. If you're looking for a sound designer for an electronic music production, then bringing in a recording engineer with a focus on recording orchestral music may not work for you. Understand that no one person can do everything, and find the person that best suits your production needs.

You now understand who will handle these roles; let's now discuss how they will do this, along with some prerequisites for doing so. I explain the prerequisites for two reasons: (1) If you want to find someone to fill one of these roles, you'll know what to look for, and (2) if you want to do it yourself, you'll know what you need to do it.

Musical Instruments When it comes to sound design, this is an art form that takes place in both pre-production and post-production, pre-production being any time before the documentation of the musical instrument into an audio recording. Before this moment of documentation, the sound design implemented for the instrument may be the most important moment of the whole production. Imagine recording a full song with an out-of-tune instrument; this is exactly what will happen to a performance or recording with no sound design involved. This doesn't need to be a complicated task; it can be as simple as understanding a few things about musical instruments:

- The type of instrument
- How to tune the instrument

- The brands and makers for the instrument
- The materials of the instrument
- Additional details for each and every instrument in your production

With these things in mind, it is possible to design the sound of an instrument just by adjusting the instrument itself. If you have an instrument that sounds too bright, throw a blanket over it; if you have a string instrument that is too dull, change the strings. There are many ways to go about this, and the simple truth is that the more a sound designer understands instruments, the better he or she can manipulate them. And that brings us to a final point: sound designing an instrument is not solely about making the instrument sound "perfect." It's about making the instrument sound the best it can for the production. This can mean making the instrument sound as natural as possible, or as abstract as you'd like. The sound designer has the ability to take any instrument to any depths desired to meet the production requirements.

Production Takeaway: "Put in a little extra time to make something sound great, as opposed to putting in a lot more time to fix what's not." This is a producer's creed regarding sound design. Of course we can make things sound better in post-production, but we can't *always* make things sound better in post. If something sounds good from the beginning, it will *always* sound good in the end. Let's look at some prerequisites, pros, and cons for sound designing with musical instruments.

- Prerequisites:
    * Musical instrument tuning experience: five to ten years is recommended for quality results
    * Musical sense for hearing timbre: five to ten years is recommended for quality results
- Pros:
    * Possible with any instrument
    * Easily learned through experience
    * No need to play the instrument you are adjusting
- Cons:
    * Takes time to understand what works through experience
    * Limited to the sounds of the instrument

Audio Processing   Audio processing is an incredible way to transform the sound of a musical instrument or any audio signal into a completely new sound. Simply put, there are sound processing modules to which you can send sound, and when that sound comes out, it is completely different. Audio processing is so common, that it is 99.9 percent guaranteed to be part of the production of your music if you are recording in any way. To get the best results from audio processing, it's very helpful to understand four common categories:

1. Dynamic effects
2. Distortion effects
3. Space effects
4. Modulation effects

There are also many combinations of these listed effects.

Many DAWs come equipped with software audio effects right from installation, and you can immediately utilize a variety of audio effects for your own productions. If you do not have a grasp on these already, it can be very helpful to bring someone to your production team who does, to give you the best advice on the types of audio effects that will move your production forward.

Production Takeaway: If you are in need of audio effect processing, then it is very helpful to understand the types of audio effects available to get the job done, or find someone that understands them to help you. Let's review some prerequisites, pros, and cons for sound designing with audio processing.

- Prerequisites:
  - Audio signal flow knowledge: two to five years is recommended for quality results
  - Musical sense for hearing timbre: five to ten years is recommended for quality results

- Pros:
  - * Easily transfer knowledge of audio effect parameters and signal flow across multiple audio effects
  - * No need for music theory knowledge to sound design with audio effects
  - * Extremely high limits based on your own creativity
- Cons:
  - * Years of practice is required for quality results
  - * Some audio effects are unattainable for various reasons (cost, size, discontinued, etc.)
  - * Some audio effects are limited to a specific set of parameters and results

Synthesizers Sound design with synthesizers have become increasingly popular since the early 1960s up until today. A synthesizer is essentially an electronic musical instrument that generates audio signals shaped and modulated by components such as filters, envelopes, and low-frequency oscillators. Today, synthesizers are so powerful that we can craft the sound of almost any string instrument, any horn or wind instrument, even human vocals, and these sounds all start from a single shaped sound wave. To get the best results from synthesis, it's very helpful to understand four common categories:

1. Subtractive synthesis
2. FM synthesis
3. Granular synthesis
4. Wavetable synthesis

There are many others constantly in development as well.

Many DAWs come equipped with software synthesizers ready to go right from installation, and you can immediately hear the difference in sound textures for each type of synthesizer. If you do not have a grasp on these already, it can be very helpful to bring someone to your production team who does, to give advice on the types of synthesizer to use help your production in the best way possible.

Producer Takeaway: It is extremely common for music producers to feel the need to learn how to play and/or understand the signal flow of a synthesizer, and I want to say that this is not a necessity. By all means, if you have interest in this, learn it; if you simply want to learn to help your work by knowing more, learn it. But it's not mandatory to understand how synthesizers work to produce a song. Remember, if you are in need of synthesis design, then it is very helpful to understand the types of synthesis available to get the job done, or find someone that understands them. Let's look at some prerequisites, pros, and cons for sound designing with audio processing.

- Prerequisites:
  * Synthesizer signal flow knowledge: two to five years is recommended for quality results
  * Musical sense for hearing timbre: five to ten years is recommended for quality results
- Pros:
  * Easily transfer knowledge of synthesis across multiple synthesizers
  * No need for music theory knowledge to sound design synthesizers
  * Extremely high limits based on your own creativity
- Cons:
  * Years of practice is required for quality results
  * Some synthesizers are unattainable for various reasons (cost, size, discontinued, etc.)
  * Some synthesizers are limited to a specific range and voices of timbres

Recording   Audio and MIDI recording is in the best place ever. If you have a song idea, you can record it on your phone in seconds, and it actually sounds great. If you want to record a full orchestra, you can do this on your laptop. If you want to record a Grammy-winning record, this is possible from your bed (literally—the Grammy Producer of the Year in 2020 recorded in his bedroom, with the vocalist sitting on his bed). Because of this, it's very easy to forget where we came from and that, before our laptops and smart phones, we needed recording studios and pre-amps and microphones to record music. Even though the art of recording has advanced, the theory of signal flow and audio processing has remained the same (with a few updates here and there), allowing producers of all ages to jump into a production and bring in a team from any recording era to bring out the best musical performances and document these in the best way possible.

Production Takeaway: If your production is in need of documentation, whether that be audio recording or MIDI, there are a great number of tools available to do this. So, whether you need to record something on your smart phone or laptop, all the way to a professional studio, the great thing is that the main concepts behind the way the technology works is very similar. When it comes to stepping things up with gear that you are not familiar with, or you are really looking for a higher level of color and authenticity with analog gear, this may be a great time to bring in someone with audio recording experience. If you do not have the experience, there is definitely an audio recording engineer out there to help you get this job done. Let's review some prerequisites, pros, and cons for recording.

- Prerequisite:
  - Musical instrument recording experience: five to ten years is recommended for quality results
  - Musical sense for hearing timbre: five to ten years is recommended for quality results
- Pros:
  - Gear is easily accessible in mobile or studio locations
  - Easily learned through experience
  - No need to play the instruments you are recording

- Cons:
    * Takes time to understand what works through experience
    * Limited to the sounds of a recording
    * Some recording gear is unattainable for various reasons (cost, size, discontinued, etc.)

APPLICATION TO YOUR PRODUCTIONS

When it comes to sound design, trusting your ears is an incredibly important factor not only in planning how something will sound, but deciding when you have arrived at a point of completion. Take for example a student of mine, whose goal was to release a hard-hitting techno production. This student had a few years of production experience but was hitting roadblocks when it came to the sound design of the instruments in his production. These roadblocks were halting the production process, as this student's order was heavily based on writing the music composition following inspiration from the sounds he chose to work with. The longer it took him to choose the sounds for the production, the longer it took to start writing a musical composition and arrangement.

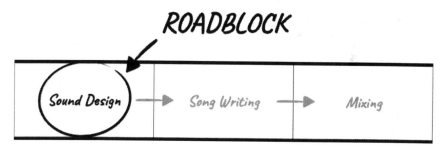

From my perspective, it was honestly difficult at first to pick out what the issue was. I was listening to the music while viewing my student's project file, and although something sounded "off," everything looked fine inside of his DAW. The project was organized, the tracks were labeled, and through the organization, the issue was unveiled. Among the thirty or so tracks in the session, there were three tracks labeled "Kick Low," "Kick Body," and "Kick Top"; these tracks were playing three different kick drums at the same time, which I'll say is not only normal, but very common. For the most part, I *preferred* to layer these kick elements together in a song. In theory, everything made sense, though I needed to check things further. I muted two of the kicks, and the moment I did that, it was as if a moment of clarity in the music appeared. It sounded like I had hit a magic switch, and the song "worked." My student heard this clarity as well, and asked what I did. I explained that I simply removed the other kick drums. The student then asked if new kick drums should be added to replace the ones that were removed. I asked him again how it sounded, and he did not know—he was torn. He *knew* that it sounded fine, but he was *convinced* that it wasn't perfect because of what he had trained himself to understand about needing to add *more*. It wasn't that he didn't know what sounded good; he just didn't trust his own ears, even when he liked the way it sounded. He would choose the "best way in theory" to do things, such as "layer three kick drums," no matter the scenario. I then explained something that changed the way this student viewed sound design: If you combine two kick drums together, and then record those kick drums to a new track, you then have a new kick drum that is only one audio recording.

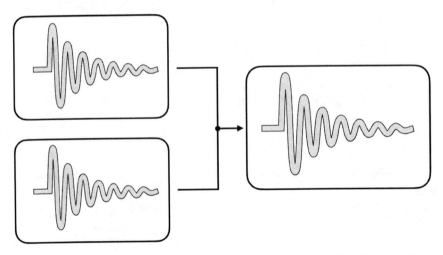

So in theory, would you now need to layer that sound with two other kick drums to make it sound more full? The student knew exactly where this was going. And he immediately learned that it's not about layering, it's not about following a "system" that worked in the past—it's about following your ears, and trusting what works. In fact, if you're using audio samples, you don't always know how many times or how many layers are recorded into that single audio sample. That one sample may already have all of the layers you need. That being said, you need to trust what you have based on your own ears and the technology available in your tools (e.g., frequency visualizers).

This student ended up cutting the number of tracks used almost by half, removing unneeded layers of sounds that were included due to a lack of trust in his own ears. Of course there are times where layering works great, and this was what the student learned as not only a producer, but as a sound designer deep in the weeds of the sound designing process. Here's an exercise we did together, to make this happen. This is similar to the exercise in Method #4, where the student pinpoints a moment in the sound design and recording process where a roadblock was occurring, and whether that student needed to either improve his or her own techniques, or involve someone else to handle this role. This exercise is focused on:

1. Writing a goal
2. Writing a problem in the sound design and recording process that created a roadblock to that goal
3. Writing two possible routes to fix this problem, either on your own or with a team
4. Writing the name(s) of the person that will handle this role.

Let me show you a few examples of solving sound design and recording problems through desire on your own, with a team, or with devices. The more specific you can be with your problem, the better you can find a solution. For example, instead of stating a problem as "I don't know anything about sound design," dig deeper into something more specific such as "I don't know how to create a deep bass kick drum."

Goal: Release a techno track for the club.

1. **Problem:** I don't know how to create a deep bass kick drum that rumbles a club.
   a. Self desire: I want to learn more about sound design.
   b. Team desire: I want to include a sound designer on my team.

2. **Problem:** I don't know how to create wide synth basses that rumbles a club.

   a. **Self desire:** I want to learn more about sound design.

   b. **Team desire:** I want to include a sound designer on my team.

3. **Problem:** I don't know how to use a DAW well enough to sound design.

   a. **Self desire:** I want to learn more about my DAW.

   b. **Team desire:** I want to include someone with DAW and sound design experience on my team.

Exercise

For this exercise, write down at least a dozen things that you are saying or thinking as you're facing an issue that is creating a roadblock in your sound design and recording workflow, or something you imagine could become an obstacle in the future. Then, determine whether this is something *you* desire to solve on your own, or a *team member* desires to solve for you. Then, write down what this desire would be, and specify who will handle this role.

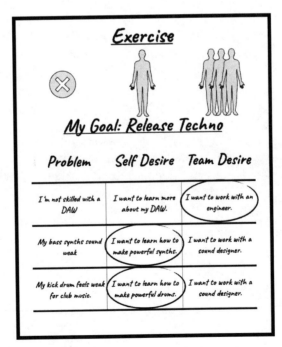

When it comes to sound design, the answers are always clearly visible and may take time to figure out with your own ears, or with the help of a mentor to unveil the answers for you. In Method #8: "Your Mentor," you will be introduced to both formal and informal learning methods that will guide and support your development as a producer. You are encouraged to revisit this method's exercise after you develop your knowledge and experience with sound design and reflect on how different your answers may be from where they are now.

6

MIXING AND MASTERING

There was a day when everything clicked, the process all made sense, and I cleared a roadblock that allowed me to achieve my goals for the final steps of the production process. I felt as if I hacked the system, as if there was a secret road to success that I opened up, and this discovery led to the start of my career as an electronic music producer. Here's how it started.

There was a time when I believed that I needed to do everything on my own. The naive younger version of myself as an electronic music producer needed to push through every step of the process, or it wasn't "my own." I can't even tell you where I learned this, although I truly believed it to be the case, even with my background as a musician in a band with a dedicated mixing and mastering engineer on our records. This younger version of myself did not make the connection that this could also be the case for my own path as an electronic music producer. I was naive, but I was tenacious, and this tenacity to push through an obstacle that was blocking the path to my goal is an experience I would not replace for the world, even though I am now comfortable allowing other professionals to handle this role in my process. This roadblock was mixing and mastering, and there finally came a day when it all made sense and everything clicked—I was able to understand how it all worked, allowing me to achieve the results I desired.

Like many other electronic music producers, or recording engineers, I was listening to countless records and countless references to "perfect mixes," and I would inevitably compare my own work as being subpar. It was almost impossible to figure out why, and how to get my mixes to sound the way they did on these professional records. This deficit stood in the way of my goal; I had a desire: to release my own original electronic music with Bosphorus Underground, a minimal techno label based out of Istanbul. I have come to love minimal techno, especially from artists from the likes of this label, and my goal was to release one of my songs with the label. I believed it would change my life forever, and put everything I had into making this happen. I simply needed to overcome this mixing and mastering roadblock.

I was mixing in my bedroom at the time, and got to where I knew exactly how I was mixing. I understood that I wasn't in a professional studio, I knew that I didn't have million-dollar monitors, and I knew that I had a single laptop with only enough CPU to handle a limited number of heavy-duty plugins. I knew my limits, and this was important when moving forward with my production. I spent hours, days, nights striving for the perfect mixdown. I spent so much time trying to make everything work the best it could, but the truth was that it never sounded quite right. It always sounded like it was "overmixed" or "overproduced," and I was always attempting to fix something, leading me down a rabbit hole of editing, equalizing, and sculpting until I had nothing left—and it sounded even worse than when I started.

And here was the problem: I spent years trying to fix things that sounded terrible; I tried to make terrible things sounds great, and that was the issue. I believed that this is what mixing was. It wasn't until I tried a new approach: sampling some of my favorite songs. I sampled kick drums, I sampled bass hits, I samples hi-hats, I sampled things that I knew worked, because someone else used them. I felt like I was stealing gold, although I was reusing sounds in a new context (which soothed my conscience).

It was then, as I went about my process as I normally did and wrote a song with these newly sampled tools, that I realized I didn't need to do much with sound design, as these items already sounded great. I touched up a few things here and there, and glued the sounds together with some effects, but nothing crazy. Then it was time to mix—my kryptonite as a producer, a step I could never complete. Mixing was the barrier stopping me from reaching my goal of releasing on the labels I aspired to, the stage of the process that I couldn't surpass. But this time, it was different. I adjusted some levels; I adjusted some equalizers; I adjusted a few things here and there, and—that was it. Everything worked. It was the first time that everything simply *worked*. And I learned what mixing was: it was the balance. Mixing didn't need to be the carving up or manipulation of my song, it simply needed to be *balanced*. If I could hear everything I needed, and all parts sound great without much or any work at all, then the mixdown will naturally find its way. I ended up recording the vocals of my friend on my iPhone, added this into the song, and I applied the same thought process—make his vocals sound the best I can, and they will find their way in. And they did. I uploaded the song to Soundcloud and YouTube, and it was my most popular release at the time; it was the first time I uploaded something to the internet, and over 50,000 people listened to it, which was mind-blowing. It wasn't millions of people, but it was clarity, and it was confirmation that my new approach worked, that I could do this.

I went back into the studio (my bedroom) and started from the ground up once again, although this time I kept in mind where I started the last time: with the best sounds I could find. I found the best samples, and I performed the best sound design possible to individual sounds for the sole reason of making each sound "work"—not to oversculpt or manipulate because I could, but only if I *needed* to—all before even imagining the mixdown. I eventually completed and sent this new song to an artist named Mark Dekoda, who started his own label, on which my first minimal techno was released. This song eventually gained traction and introduced me to some great friends and future label mates. One in particular is Chris Lawyer, who was releasing on Bosphorus Underground at the time; we've since written and produced many projects along with discussing the philosophy of production over countless nights, leading to releases of my own work on Bosphorus Underground, the label I strongly wanted to be a part of, along with Chris's own label, Naschkatze Underground. This realization of my production process was a stepping stone and the beginning of my career as an electronic music producer.

PRINCIPLES

It's hard for most of us to remember, and sometimes difficult for use to even conceptualize that we once created music very differently than the way we do it today—creating music on our mobile devices, computers, or electronic sequencers. The process of "mixing a song" is continuously changing with advances in technology, and it's important for music producers to stay on top of the options available, along with understanding how technology brought us to this point and how powerful it can be to understand not only mixing and mastering, but the tools used. In this method we'll discuss two common ways to mix and master music, along with how to choose the best team member or individual to work with if you want to oversee this process on your own.

Getting Involved with Mixing and Mastering

In Method #2, you learned about mixing and mastering from a bird's-eye view, but in this method we'll break down the typical roles for mixing and mastering, along with common practices for mixing and mastering your own music. Let's start off with the roles.

Mixing Engineer   # Mastering Engineer

Two common roles involved with the mixing and mastering process of a music production are mixing engineer and mastering engineer. You may have heard these titles before, but if you haven't, here is a brief explanation in case you're looking for someone to fill this role for your own production.

Mixing engineer: The role of a mixing engineer is to combine and balance all of the difference sonic elements of a recorded piece of music into a single audio documentation.

Mastering engineer: The role of a mastering engineer is to take an audio recording that has previously been mixed and make final adjustments to this piece of recorded music as the final step of the music production process.

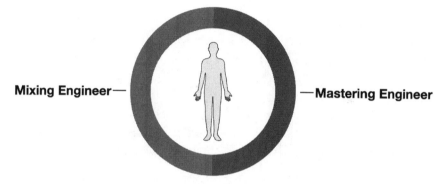

There is no rule that these roles are to be filled by two separate individuals. It is common to find a mixing engineer who is also a mastering engineer, although this is not always the case. In the end, it's not about finding a person who is capable of handling both of these roles, but how well a person performs each role.

For example, a common goal for a mixing engineer is to balance the recorded audio for a music project, so the listener can easily focus on specific points within the music. The mixing engineer also has creative freedom to push the limit of what he or she intends the listener to focus on, creating a new way to not only mix music, but engage with it as a listener. A common goal for a mastering engineer is to complete the production process; to add the final touches—the icing on the cake, you might say—on the final mixdown, with a mix and master that translates well across a wide range of listening sources such as speakers, headphones, and other devices.

Producer Takeaway: If you are not handling the mixing and mastering portion of a project on your own, you will most likely be reaching out to someone with some or all these talents. It's up to you to figure out what your production needs, and find the person that will push your production forward.

You now understand who can handle these roles within your production; let's now discuss how they will do this, along with some prerequisites for doing so. I present the prerequisites for two reasons: (1) If you want to find someone to do it, you'll know what to look for, and (2) if you want to do it yourself, you'll know what you need.

Digital Audio Workstation   A digital audio workstation (DAW) is the most common form of audio recording, editing, and mixing software available today. Simply put, a DAW is an application installed on a computer or laptop that offers multitrack recording and playback, audio and MIDI editing, audio and MIDI effects processing, digital instruments, live performance tools, and even more. Depending on the software of choice, you may have access to unlimited tracks, thousands of instrument and audio effect presets, and everything you might need to mix a professional level mixdown. DAWs have become the industry standard for not only recording and editing music, but mixing and mastering as well.

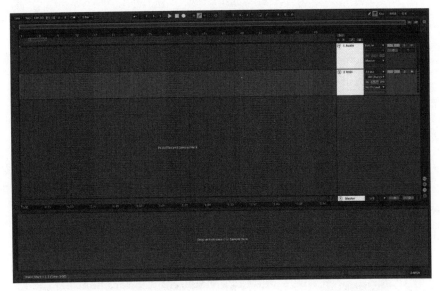

Producer Takeaway: When it comes to using a DAW, there is no correct choice as far as which is "the best" DAW. Although there are slight differences between each DAW, understanding which type works best for your needs is important before jumping into purchasing a full version. The great thing about most DAWs is that most offer a free trial session so that you can try out the software and test its features. I recommend that you try out all the software you can before purchasing a DAW, so you can decide which works best for you. Another route is to simply ask for reviews through your personal contacts, your mentors, or based on recommendations from an admired music creator who uses a particular DAW. Here are a few common DAWs today:

- Ableton Live
- Apple Logic
- Avid Pro Tools
- Steinberg Cubase
- Image-Line FL Studio
- Apple GarageBand

- Prerequisites:
  * Audio recording and editing experience: five to ten years is recommended for quality results
  * MIDI recording and editing experience: five to ten years is recommended for quality results
  * Audio effects knowledge: Intermediate to advanced understanding is desired for quality results
  * MIDI effects knowledge: Intermediate to advanced understanding is desired for quality results
- Pros:
  * Affordable prices for the level of power
  * Full studio inside your laptop
  * Extremely common for sharing projects for collaborations
  * Relatively flat learning curve
- Cons:
  * Some DAWs are unattainable for various reasons (cost, operating system, etc.)
  * Some DAWs are limited to a specific computer operating system
  * If you collaborate with others on different DAWs, then you cannot share projects

* Your ability to use a DAW does not make you "better" at mixing music; this is simply a tool to produce music.

Mixing Console   When it comes to understanding where the DAW came from, a mixing console is a good place to start. A mixing console is a digital device for combining and balancing various paths of audio signals; simply put, it is a device for mixing your music. Unlike a DAW, a mixing console is not generally used to cut and edit your music, but is focused only on the "mixing," the balancing of the instruments and tracks within the song.

Producer Takeaway: Just as with a DAW, when it comes to using a mixing console, there is no correct choice in terms of the "best" console. However, there are differences between each type of console, and understanding which works best for your projects is definitely something to check out before jumping into purchasing one. Some consoles may have built-in effects, parameters, or even an overall color or tone that is produced from the console itself. The great thing about most consoles is that they are often found in professional music studios, meaning you can most likely rent out a studio and use its mixing console if needed. If there are any consoles that you absolutely enjoy working with, you may be able to continue using the studio that owns the console, or consider purchasing one for your own use.

- Prerequisites:
  * Audio recording and editing experience: five to ten years is recommended for quality results
  * Audio effects knowledge: Intermediate to advanced understanding is desired for quality results
  * Signal flow and routing knowledge: five to ten years is recommended for quality results
- Pros:
  * Original sound with regard to the chosen console
  * No need for computer space
  * Hands-on feel for mixing
  * Likely to age well through time
- Cons:
  * Some mixing consoles are unattainable for various reasons (cost, size, etc.)
  * Some analog consoles are difficult to repair, especially if the pieces are vintage
  * Your ability to use an analog console does not make you "better" at mixing; this is simply a tool to produce music.
  * Can be difficult to master

APPLICATION TO YOUR PRODUCTIONS

This method is applicable to producers who are interested in refining their mixing skills, or interested in including a team member to mix and master their projects. Take my student Chase, introduced in Method #1, whose goal was to release an EP *by the end of the summer*. Chase included a mixing engineer on his team to complete his project, although this doesn't mean that Chase didn't need to learn anything about mixing—in fact, the opposite was true. As a producer who needed to bring in a mixing engineer, the more Chase understood about mixing, the more likely he will choose the most suitable engineer and also how to communicate what he wants the engineer to achieve and deliver. I told Chase that if he wanted to bring in an engineer, he would need to know how to answer the following:

- How do you want the mix to sound?
- How do you explain your preferred balance of each sound in the mix?
- How do you prepare your project to send to the mixing and mastering engineer?
- How do you send the project to the mixing and mastering engineer?

If Chase wanted to add a great engineer to his team, this knowledge, along with many other tips, are essential. I explained how balancing works, and how frequencies, dynamics, width, depth, and overall soundscaping play a role in the mixdown process.

I then explained how he could use shapes and drawings to represent what he wants the overall balance to sound like, for example, when he wants certain instruments or tracks to move to the front of the mix or to the back of the mix, or when to create space and ambience in the mix. We discussed how to level out his project, giving enough head room for the engineer to work with, and how to write detailed notes on exactly what he wants to hear in order to deal with as few revisions as possible.

Chase was able to get everything he needed to the engineer and moved forward with two or three revisions, until he had a final version of the song that sounded great. Here's an exercise we did together to achieve this. Chase went to his project and listened carefully to what he needed to achieve, and he made notes as detailed as he could write down, along with drawing out an overall image of the sound he wanted to present in the mix. This exercise focuses on:

1. Writing a sonic desire for the music
2. Writing a detailed description of how this will sound
3. Drawing a template of where this sound will lay in the mix
4. Deciding whether this will be achieved alone, or with a team member.

Let me show you a few examples of moving forward with your mixdown on your own or with a team.

1. **Problem:** I don't know how to balance my tracks.
   a. **Self desire:** I want to learn more about mixing.

    b. Team desire: I want to include a mixing engineer on my team.
2. **Problem:** I don't know how make the sub bass rumble hard without overpowering the full song.
    a. Self desire: I want to learn more about mixing.
    b. Team desire: I want to include a mixing engineer on my team.
3. **Problem:** I don't know how make the vocals shine as the main focal point of my song.
    a. Self desire: I want to learn more about mixing.
    b. Team desire: I want to include a mixing engineer on my team.

Exercise

For this exercise, write down at least a dozen things that you are saying or thinking as you face an issue that is creating a roadblock in your sound design and recording workflow, or something you imagine could be a future obstacle. Determine whether this is something *you* desire to solve on your own, or a *team member* desires to solve for you. Then, write what this desire would be, and who will handle this role.

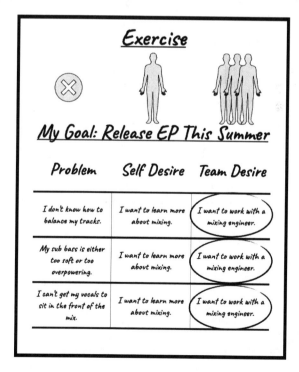

Attempt to draw a visual of your mixdown; this is an incredibly useful approach to sharing your creative vision of sound with others through images. As discussed in Method #1, a major issue when working with a team is miscommunication; this exercise provides a strategy to solve this issue through additional approaches to sharing creative thoughts, such as drawing and other visualizations.

III

REFLECTION AND DEVELOPMENT

In this section you will dive into two methods that will guide you on a path of reflection and development of your own production experience, skills, and knowledge.

1. Each method begins with a story of a true personal experience related to the topic and learning experiences provided.
2. This story then leads into principles for you to take away from these experiences.
3. This is followed by a story of a true personal experience with my students, where these principles were applied.
4. Each method concludes with an exercise for you to do to improve your own music production skill sets.

7

MODERN PROBLEMS
AND SOLUTIONS

I spent a few years living in Tokyo, Japan, and during this time I've met an incredible number of artists, producers, and creatives I'm proud to call my friends. These friends were either passing through the country on music tours or promotional events, or simply taking time off to relax and explore a new country, like I have done myself. I travelled to Japan on a music tour, and ended up staying there for a couple of years, purely because I enjoyed the country so much. I enjoyed not only Japanese history, but the mindset and discipline of the culture; the Japanese appreciation of art, creativity, and the willpower to become great at your craft. During my time in Japan, and with each new friend I met there, I had conversations that would forever change the way I produce music. These conversations were sometimes even more powerful than hands-on music production, and through these conversations I learned that there is no correct way to produce music. I learned that each and every producer I met—some with mega-hit songs, millions of plays, and millions of fans around the world; some with a small fan base, but absolutely beautiful productions—we all had different ways of going about our own production process while still meeting in the middle on the foundational roots that drive a production forward.

A particular conversation I had one day not only changed my outlook on producing, but solidified my theory; this was a conversation with two other producers which soon revealed a topic I have had not only with music producers, but creatives in general. This conversation was so liberating that I had the same discussion with about ten other highly respected creatives, and all agreed with my idea, which is based on two points of creation: the first is to choose your tools and then, based on your tools, create whatever you want.

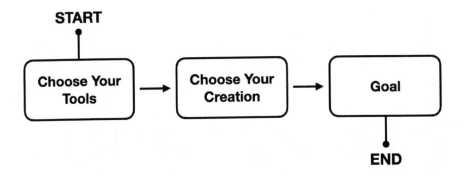

Whereas the second point is to choose what you want to create, and then obtain the tools to make it happen. The second one is more logical. Say you woke up in a room you've never been in before, and you needed to escape. What's the first thing you would do? Look around the room for a way out, or look in your bag to see what tools can help you get out? The logical answer is to look around the room; there may be a hole in the wall, or a window, and you wouldn't even need any tools. If you look in your bag, you may find many great tools, but those things may not be

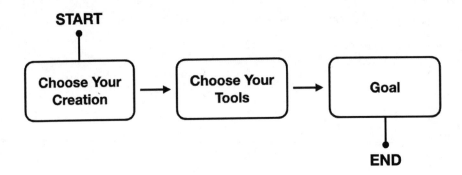

relevant to getting you out of the room. It's the same thing with production: you could have all of the tools in the world, although if you don't need them, then you may simply be jumping down a rabbit hole of using this stuff for no reason. It's more logical to decide what you want to do first, and then use the tools.

So, which is better? Which is more efficient? This is what I was stuck on before having these conversations, and the truth was that I didn't know. Sometimes I would know what I wanted, and other times I dug around my tools for inspiration. And I learned that there may be a logical way to achieve something, although music production is not always going to be a logical process. You may need inspiration from your tools to create, and that's one way of going about it. You may need to open your computer and survey your tools to see what you have, and then play around until something inspirational happens. I don't think there's a better or a worse way, and the creatives with whom I have had this discussion agree.

PRINCIPLES

I can share personal preferences on having too many or too few tools, and I can share comments on being a master of one or a jack of all trades, although in the end it's really about simply making something work. I personally don't like having a lot of tools; I prefer to understand how each one of my tools works, and learning how to do everything I possibly can with the limited number of tools I have. Someone else, however, may think the other way—they may love having more tools and not understanding how they work, but enjoy playing around and seeing what comes out, and using the inspiration of the unknown to create music.

There is no right way to create. Those who create music understand that all ways are okay, and it's about making the best of what we have. No matter what comes into play, there are key points that fit both of these paths. When it comes to creativity, it is about retrieving your ideas, understanding where the end of your production leads, understanding how to limit or make the most of your gear, knowing when something is perfect, or when you should be creating more or less. These are all points that I have encountered as a producer and as a friend of many other creative people who all have the same thoughts across a wide span of creative fields. The truth is that there are still problems to solve in the modern world, no matter how great everything may be idealistically and technologically. Yet there are solutions to these roadblocks as well.

Creativity

Creativity—or the lack of it—is something many people deal with, and I can assure you that it's not some form of magic a person is simply born with. Creativity is something you can learn to control over time. Although you can control how to direct your creativity, the truth is that sometimes you cannot control when creativity arrives. Sometimes creativity hits at moments when you least expect it, and these moments may be detrimental to the delivery of a production. For example, you may be in the final mixing phase for a song, and you get struck by an idea or inspiration, just one night before the song will be sent to the mastering engineer. As discussed in Method #3, you as a producer need to make a choice: is this idea worth recording? It this idea worth bringing a singer in? Is this idea worth redesigning the other elements to make it work? Is it worth the time, energy, and resources to commit to? The answers to these questions are up to the producer. Do you ignore this great idea, save it for another time, or use it right away? There is no correct answer. You as a producer will come across these moments; the truth is that you cannot always control when you will be creative. However, as creatives, we can do our best to enable this creativity. Here are a few tips for enabling creativity, either just before or at the exact moment it's needed.

- Create in an environment that inspires you. This can be anything from creating a cozy environment, to adjusting the lighting and mood. If you are relaxed in nature, try taking a trip somewhere than can trigger creative thoughts.
- Try not to be *too* organized, and simply let ideas run, even if they don't seem controlled or coherent at the time. When you go back to them, you may find gold in the rough.
- Experience the emotions you are writing. If you are creating sad or any other type of emotional music, try viewing some other sad

creations, whether a movie, a painting, poetry, or other art form. Observing how other art forms communicate emotion can help you understand how to translate them into your own work.

- Remake. Don't be afraid to take influences from others. Remember, there is a difference between copying and inspiring; it can be a fine line, although feel free to make that call. Mimicking other music you hear, or other artists you see, will teach you how to do the things you want to do through trial, error, practice, and experience.

Once you understand how to do those things, take similar ideas and shape them in a new way for yourself.

Short-Term Ideas

The loss of spontaneous ideas is unfortunately one of the most common, yet most basic problems of being a creator, meaning unexpected ideas appear in absolutely unplanned places, and are forgotten moments later. Have you ever had a great idea in the shower, and once you got out, the idea was gone? Have you been on a train or in your car with an amazing idea, only to have your idea vanish by the time you arrived at your destination? These ideas are similar to short-term memories, which may stay in your brain one moment and vanish as quickly as they appeared. Because this is such a common issue, it may actually be the simplest to solve. Here are suggested solutions to forgetting ideas coming out of nowhere.

- Always keep a mobile recording device handy, whether a phone or some type of digital recorder. A means to record your thoughts at any given moment is essential to remembering ideas that appear spontaneously. A waterproof recording device, or a waterproof smart phone case or something to keep your device dry is a bonus, as you'll be able to record ideas while in the shower, during a workout, or out in the rain.
- This one is not for everybody, but as you learned in Method #4, musical notation is a great way to document your ideas without the use of audio recording devices. If you know how to read and write

music, a notepad can be an essential documenting tool for lyrics, melodies, or rhythmic ideas.

- There are many song recognition applications that will not only record the audio you hear, but reveal the name and title of the music as well. There are many times when you hear a song in public—in a shopping center, a restaurant, or at a public event—that can inspire you to create something new, but unfortunately you may not know the name of the song or artist. Relistening to this song later on could possibly trigger that inspiration again, so utilizing an app such as Shazam will share and save the names and artists of many songs for later listening.

Your Final Steps

A very common problem with a music project is the order of the production. Although there are various routes to go around a production, there is always one place a production will lead to: the mixing and mastering process. No matter where you start, the production will end with mixing and mastering, even if you don't make it that far. If you don't do the mixing and mastering, then your song is simply balanced the way it was left, which in the end is *the balance* of the production. Understanding this simple ideas allows a producer to avoid getting worked up over the mixing and mastering of a song, knowing that it's going to be the final step. You may want to make things sounds great from the beginning; I know that a great sound may inspire you to create even more, and that is okay. You can do that— mixing early in the process is fine, if you know what you're doing. My only piece of advice is to treat any early mixing as "sound design" and "balancing from a bird's-eye view." It's not getting

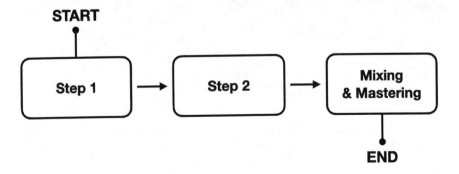

into the details of the mix and the master, but simply keeping things in balance, which is fine to do. The main takeaway here is to be aware that you will revisit this step at some point, so if you can hold off on polishing until the end, it's definitely worth doing so. In fact, it's worth throwing this into a whole new project, possibly even gaining a new set of ears, either someone else's, or even your own ears after a break from the music. Some people like keeping the flow and being within the project, while for others, taking a break and then mixing and mastering from a "fresh" point of view is helpful to regain focus on project goals. The process is up to you, and knowing that these tasks will be revisited at the end allows you to make the choice of balancing as you go, or saving this until the final moments of your production.

The Problem of Accessibility

One common problem in music production today is not really that terrible, but it can be dangerous for your growth. Think of the saying, "jack of all trades, master of none." There is so much gear out there today, and it's so accessible that it's very easy to download the latest app, the latest instrument, the latest audio effect, and forget about the ones you already own. Is this bad? No, it's important to be up-to-date on what's new, but this doesn't mean forget about what you have—or more importantly, what you *need*. Let me explain this using something known as a "T model."

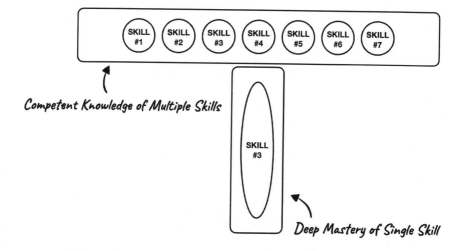

The T model showcases the understanding of a wide variety of skills and tools: instruments, audio effects, systems, and processes. However, choose one or even a select few to really learn, really focus on, really understand, really *master*. This understanding will make you an extremely valuable player, and you will not need the next piece of gear to make up for something you may lack. Remember, you're a producer. You have options and team members; you don't *need* to be great at everything, but if you are, it's because you *want* to be great. Again, I'm not here to stop you from being great at everything, but imagine being great at mixing music with a pair of speakers you really understand. It doesn't matter how much they cost, it doesn't matter what brand they are. The thing is, you know how they sound, and how to make things sound great through them. If you are constantly switching speakers, you will be constantly adjusting to learn what works, and you may never become efficient enough to master the trade. This goes for sports as well, and for anything involving focus on a skill. As a producer, it's important to find your focus, whether it's a specific topic covered in this book or simply as an overseer of productions. Think about where you want to focus your deeper learning, and this will likely benefit you greatly in the end.

Minimizing the Gap to Perfection

Striving for perfection is the death of all producers. Here's the truth behind perfection: it is great to set a goal of perfection, and expect to fall short. This may sound negative, but let me put perfection into perspective, allowing you as a producer to strive for it—and get better, by not reaching it. Shoot for the stars! You're not going to reach the stars—they're millions of light years away—but if you jump about ten feet in the air, you're reaching towards perfection.

Let's break perfection down into three categories: time, effort, and probability. And let's use a crazy example, such as making a billion dollars. Is that far-fetched? No, I don't think so, anything is possible. Let's break down this goal:

Time: I want to make a billion dollars, *immediately*.
Effort: I want to make a billion dollars, with *no effort*.
Probability: I want to make a billion dollars, with *100 percent chance of success*.

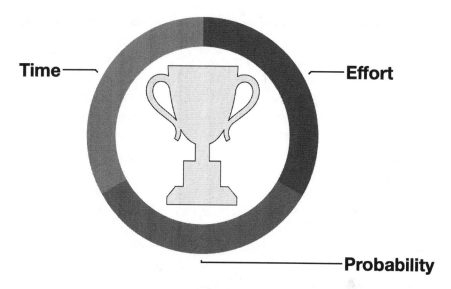

Time —   — Effort

———————— Probability

Let's say that at the snap of your fingers, with no effort, with a definite guarantee, you have a billion dollars. This is perfection at its finest. So, is this possible? Very unlikely, like our goal of perfection. So, anything we do will push us closer to perfection.

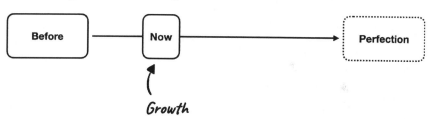

| Before | Now | Perfection |

Growth

If I'm on track to make a billion dollars in fifty years, and I am able to cut this down to forty-five years, I have just moved closer to perfection. If I plan to work twenty hours a day to make a billion dollars, and I cut this down to ten hours a day, I have just moved closer to perfection. If I went from no chance of making a billion dollars to a 1 percent chance, I have just moved closer to perfection.

As a music producer, it's very important to understand that moving toward perfection is extremely important, gratifying, and motivating, not only to improve your production skills but to become more efficient at doing it. Completing projects that are imperfect is simply a time stamp of your current experience, your current knowledge, and your current capabilities as a producer. The fear of not completing projects, not releasing products, and not achieving goals, due to not quite reaching perfection will destroy the output of a producer, but the truth is, this lack of "perfection" is very rarely observed from the outside. Someone else may regard your creations as perfect even when you do not. Others may not see all of your mistakes, but may not see where you grew from or what you were shooting for, either. All the listener has is the time stamp of where you are at that time, and what you have created as a producer.

In the end, understand that others may view your striving for perfection as perfection in its own way. Doing your best to close this gap between reality and perfection will raise this level of perceived perfection from the outside. So, how do you close this gap? Throughout this book you have learned methods for understanding each role in the production, the order of production, and the production itself. Using what you know through practice and experience will allow you to identify what you need to enhance to move your productions even closer to perfection and achieve your goals.

Quality versus Quantity

Quality verses quantity is an important topic not only in the world of music production, but all forms of content production. This is the big question of producing more music of a lower quality, or producing less music of a higher quality. This choice is completely dependent on the type of projects you are working on, so let me provide two examples, and let you decide which is the best path for you, along with a list of pros and cons for each.

An extremely common example is Producer A, who is striving for "perfection" and will not complete a song until that song is absolutely

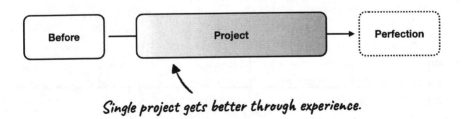

Single project gets better through experience.

perfect. It takes Producer A five years to complete and share a song with the world.

On the other hand, Producer B is also striving for perfection, although Producer B accepts the concept of striving toward perfection with every project. Producer B completes one song every month, and after two years, becomes even better through experience.

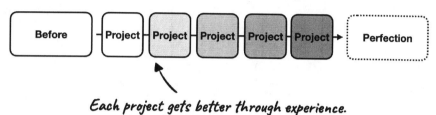

Each project gets better through experience.

In the end, Producer A has one great song, but only one song's worth of experience, and limited growth in experience. Producer B has over fifty songs, which is over fifty songs' worth of experience. Which do you think is better? Which do you prefer?

In table 7.1, you can see that the pros of prioritizing quality can lead to higher value and higher attention to detail. The cons of prioritizing quality are related to lower output of content and less project experience for yourself as a creator. On the other hand, the pros of prioritizing quantity include higher output of content and greater variety of project experience for creators. The cons of prioritizing quantity include lower value and less attention to detail.

Table 7.1. Pros and Cons of Quality versus Quantity

Quality Pros	*Quality Cons*
High(er) value	Low(er) output
More attention to detail	Less project experience
Quantity Pros	*Quantity Cons*
High(er) output	Low(er) value
More project experience	Less attention to detail

An additional factor to take into consideration is your growth. Another thing to consider is that quantity versus quality is *not always* a tradeoff. Through experience and growth, you will naturally get better and quicker at what you do. Because of this growth, you will naturally improve quality and at a greater quantity than before. When you look back on your younger self, you may notice that you don't always need to reduce the quality to produce more, because through self-growth you may be producing more than you did previously, at an even higher quality than before. Simply put, your own growth will raise both the quality and quantity of your work.

The pros and cons shown in table 7.1 relate to your current level of production, whatever this may be at the time and wherever it may be in the future. No matter your level, there will always be a balance between the two.

APPLICATION TO YOUR PRODUCTIONS

I've had the opportunity to meet and teach many students over the years through workshops and educational events around the world, including the United States, Japan, Taiwan, Hong Kong, Thailand, Indonesia, Philippines, and New Zealand. These events were so much more than simply meeting music producers and artists; I met all kinds of people, both kids and adults, who did not even speak my language but shared common goals and a love of creation. Through these events I taught not only topics related to music production but also topics such as being a leader, taking responsibility, staying creative, welcoming sensitivity to art, improving organization, and accepting disorganization. There is so much more to being a producer than music knowledge, and these topics constitute a large number of the questions I have received from students and aspiring producers during these events.

These questions not only covered technical problems and solutions, but more philosophical or sensitive knowledge such as how I knew I wanted to be a producer, how I know when a song made me feel an emotion, how I know when a project was complete, how I stay organized while traveling the world, and how I find time to balance my personal life with my creative life. These types of questions inspired me to write this book. Therefore this book not only focuses on music production knowledge, but hopefully answers questions asked by students around the world with different languages and cultures but with a common goal of creating and producing.

A recurring topic in these workshops around the world relates to the perception of music from two different perspectives: our own perspective and the listener's (audience) perspective. I did my best to showcase this topic as a point of discussion, reflection, and feedback, as this is most often the final point of delivery for our productions—the moment when a listener interacts with our work. I stressed the importance of this moment, as these interactions can find their way into our planned production goals, leading to a goal-driven production on a set path from the very start of music creation all the way to the final moment of delivery.

To demonstrate this, I would invite a volunteer to present their music project to the other participants, then open the room to feedback and comments on the volunteer's project. I asked individuals to share their feedback, and would often hear comments regarding the mix, the song writing, the sound design, and the emotion. More often than not, the volunteer would respond in defense to the feedback, explaining to the others why they made certain choices, and what their intentions were. Occasionally, a participant would simply ask a question: what the *goals* were for this project, or *why* a certain choice was made, or what type of emotion was *desired* through this production. These questions *always* led to a discussion rather than a defense in response to a comment.

This activity demonstrates a very important lesson about our music: the listeners may not have the opportunity to ask questions, or know your goals for this project, or identify the emotion that you wished to communicate. In the end, it's very likely that the listeners will simply be listening from their own perspectives, and we as producers need to do our best to demonstrate what we choose to communicate. We have the ability to communicate our intentions as best as we can, and to avoid feeling defensive about every production release.

Here is an exercise I present to my students to increase their understanding of showcasing and communicating the goals and intentions of their productions to a listener. I ask my students to do the best they can to explain the goals of their production, and find moments in the music where this goal is showcased. Write down why and what happens to achieve this goal. The more precise you can be with your choices, the clearer your future productions will communicate a clear message, and you will develop better ways to convey your message through your music in all future productions, whether you choose to incorporate this message or not. This exercise is focused on:

1. Writing a goal
2. Writing a problem that created a roadblock to that goal
3. Writing two possible routes to fix this problem, either on your own, or with a team.

Let me show you a few examples of solving problems through desire on *your own*, and with *a team* to achieve your goal.

Goal: I want to produce a hard-hitting dance song about sadness that resolves into happiness.

1. **Problem:** When people listen to my song, they say it sounds hard-hitting, but never leads to happiness.
   a. **Self desire:** I want to learn more about music theory.
   b. **Team desire:** I want to include a song writer on my team.
2. **Problem:** When people listen to my song, they say it sounds soft.
   a. **Self desire:** I want to learn more about making my song hit harder in the sound design and mixing process.
   b. **Team desire:** I want to include a sound designer or mixing engineer on my team.

Exercise

For this exercise, write down at least a dozen things you are saying or thinking as you are facing a roadblock between the projects you are creating and the response from your listeners, or something you imagine may be a future. Then, determine whether this is something *you* desire to solve on your own, or a *team member* desires to solve for you. Finally, write down that desire. This is something you should do every day. I'm always aware of the questions and statements that I am thinking as I decide how to move forward with a production of music. The truth is that most people don't see what the issues are until we stop, think, and reflect on them.

<u>Exercise</u>

<u>My Goal: Hard Emotional Dance Song (Sad to Happy)</u>

Problem	Self Desire	Team Desire
Listeners say my song is sad, and never leads to happiness.	I want to learn more about music theory.	I want to include a song writing team.
Listeners say my song sounds soft.	I want to learn more about sound design and mixing.	I want to work with a sound designer or engineer

8

YOUR MENTOR

I remember sitting in my bedroom at fourteen years old, waiting for my first drum teacher to arrive. He was a college student giving drum lessons as a part-time job, and during those lessons I learned how to syncopate my kick drum while playing a beat. I distinctly remember playing the song "Someday" by the Strokes, and adjusting the kick drum off the beat while maintaining a straight hi-hat pattern. This was my first taste of learning something *new* on the drums, something that I achieved with someone else's help, because I simply couldn't figure it out on my own. I honestly can't even tell you the name of this college student; my parents probably found him through an ad. I remember at the time that I didn't necessarily want to be who he was, but I wanted to do what he was able to do, and he helped me achieve this. This person put time and effort into helping me move toward a goal, and I learned how important this type of learning can be.

I have had many teachers throughout my life, from my first piano teacher as a ten-year-old to drum teachers throughout my teens, who all helped me achieve levels of technique and discipline for which I am extremely grateful. There is, however, a specific moment when I learned the true meaning of mentorship. It was when I was recording drums with the band I mentioned in Method #1, with a recording engineer, mixing engineer, and producer whom I greatly admired. Along with producing our group, he was a highly requested engineer, and it was during those sessions when I asked to assist him on his other projects—to simply help out, watch what he did, and learn more, as he was a busy engineer with a list of bands on his recording calendar. He kindly consented, and I soon found myself setting up microphones, wrapping cables, preparing the mixing console, and doing things that have outweighed anything I learned while audio recording in college. But the most important moments occurred when I wasn't doing anything other than sitting and watching him at work. When it was time to record, I would watch how he interacted with the bands and artists. I observed how he would explain again what needed to be done, and how to achieve a great recording. I watched how he would organize and mix his session, and saw the entire process from start to finish. It was a learning experience I could not have found anywhere else. After each session we would chat about how it all went down, what worked, and what didn't work. These sessions played an incredible role in guiding my own direction for growth as a producer, and my observations were simply a piece of the puzzle in relation to all the other forms of learning I was doing on my own to build my own knowledge, experience, and practice as a music producer.

PRINCIPLES

When it comes to learning music production, it's not always about how much you know. Just as important is how much *you have done*. Experience is a key asset to being a great producer, and the best way to learn is in the form of mentoring. There's really two ways you could go about learning: own your own, or from a mentor.

Learning on your own is great, and I truly believe it is one of the best ways to get started, as this is where your true inspiration comes from. If you purely enjoy doing something, you will do it on your own, without anybody telling you that you need to do it. It has been proven through studies that this makes you better at doing something because you are emotionally engaged in the process, allowing your brain to learn how to do it better. The drawback of this approach is that it can take an incredible amount of time, and a great deal of trial and error, to learn something. This isn't always the case, although there is a good chance that it will take longer. Now imagine you now have someone to tell you what works and what doesn't work, allowing you to minimize that trial and error. This is where a mentor comes in.

Learning from a great mentor will absolutely cut back your trial-and-error time. Mentoring will let you know what works, and more importantly, it will let you know what doesn't work even before you try something. Is this good? Of course, although there is still a downside. Because you know what doesn't work, you may not try things on your own. If you know a stove is hot, why would you touch it? If you don't know, you may touch it, get hurt, and you'll immediately learn to never do that again for the rest of your life. Touching the stove took additional time, but you learned the lesson more thoroughly than if somebody simply told you not to do it. So, the next time you want to pick something up from the stove, you will find a towel or an oven mitt and put it on. You made the choice on your own, deciding that you can still touch the stove without hurting yourself. You used your own logic and your own creativity to achieve a goal, with a solution to a problem *you* were experiencing. You built experience through your own actions, which is stronger than anything you can learn from someone else. This is similar to mentoring. You may learn quickly and efficiently, you may learn what to do and what not to do, but you are also reducing your likelihood of interacting with that stove. Of course, you don't want to get a burn, and of course you don't want to waste time, but the power of your own learning will not only solidify your knowledge, but create your own solutions to problems—like wearing the oven mitt.

In the end, there are pros and cons to learning on your own or with a mentor. A balance of both is most likely to give you the best results. Let's take a look at two types of learning, both on your own and with a mentor.

Formal Learning

Formal learning is commonly in the form of schooling, whether public or private schools from elementary to high school and later, colleges and universities. Formal learning can be in the form of group lessons or one-to-one training. We live in a time when formal learning can be accessed online as well; you could enroll in a synchronous class (in real time) or an asynchronous class (not in real time) online, which would involve video lessons and possibly group or one-to-one meetups with an instructor as a hybrid learning experience. Hybrid learning could be both in-person and online, or in-person and video. There are many paths to formal learning, including using this book as a tool for formal learning about music production. Learning can also be in the form of any multimedia including videos, books, audio, images, gifs, and other technologies being developed.

There are three common sources of formal learning about music production: video, books, and school.

Video   Video learning is an incredible source of formal learning. For years video has been a resource for connecting with the masters of a trade that you might not be exposed to in person, although you can view their knowledge by watching a recorded video, which is very helpful. This could be in the form a video series, video course, or even a stand-alone video that will teach you a single lesson about a single topic.

- Pros:
    * Countless lessons and topics provided in video form
    * Extremely reliable sources available through formal education
    * The opportunity to learn and review at your own pace
- Cons:
    * Some videos are unattainable for various reasons (cost, time, etc.)
    * Learning mainly consists of student input, with no interaction with the instructor
    * Because of the abundance of lessons, it can be difficult to know which sources to trust

Books   Books are an incredible source of formal learning. For years, books have been a resource for learning many trade skills, not only in music production but in almost every field of study. Similar to video, books are a resource for connecting you to masters of a trade that you may not have the opportunity to encounter in person, through their own knowledge documented in not only text form, but sometimes in multimedia form as well, because many books now include downloadable media content to support the content of the books with lessons, exercises, and additional material.

- Pros:
  - ⁕ Countless lessons and topics provided in book form
  - ⁕ Extremely reliable sources available through formal education
  - ⁕ The opportunity to learn and review at your own pace
- Cons:
  - ⁕ Some books are unattainable for various reasons (cost, time, etc.)
  - ⁕ Mainly consist of student input, with no interaction with the author
  - ⁕ Because of the abundance of books available, it can be difficult to know which sources to trust

School Schools are a widely popular source of music education, and in recent years, a way to learn production as well. There are many schools around the world, both in-person and online, that offer all of the tools needed to begin, make progress, and achieve your goals as a producer through guided levels—either privately on your own, or with a classroom of other students.

- Pros:
  - ⁕ Direct contact with your teacher, instructor, and mentor
  - ⁕ Extremely reliable sources available through formal education
  - ⁕ The opportunity to learn with other students at your own level
- Cons:
  - ⁕ Some schools are unattainable for various reasons (cost, time, etc.)
  - ⁕ Some schools are focused on outcomes that do not align with your own personal goals
  - ⁕ Because of the abundance of schools and programs available, it can be difficult to know which sources to trust

Informal Learning

Informal learning is commonly in the form of learning from others, whether your own circle of friends or people you don't know but are willing to share their advice. Informal learning can be anything from meeting with a group of friends, attending a community meetup or a conference discussion, and today even through online forums and social media groups. Lessons can take the form of anything from an in-person discussion to a video demonstration from a "nonprofessional" all the way to written or audio files, images, gifs, and other forms.

There are four common sources of informal learning: friends, YouTube, online resources, and seminars/webinars.

Friends   Learning from friends, colleagues, and anyone in your own inner circle is an incredible source of learning at an informal level. For any skill set, whether you are a music producer or a professional sports athlete, learning from others around you is something that not only teaches you new and creative ways to achieve results, but pushes you through teamwork and efforts to grow with others as part of a group. This could be in the form of sharing ideas learned through formal education, all the way to simply having a discussion on a topic in order to brainstorm creative ideas.

- Pros:
  * Builds motivation to grow through an enjoyable learning environment
  * Builds long-term skills through active learning
  * Increases the opportunity to be both a teacher and student to others
- Cons:
  * The person providing information is not always a trustable source
  * You are limited to your personal connections and inner circle for knowledge
  * Requires time for trial and error work to confirm results of the learning

YouTube   Similar to formal video learning, YouTube has become an incredible source of learning at an informal level. The educational content of almost any skill set in the world can be found on YouTube at no cost, to view and learn at your own convenience. Also similar to formal video content, YouTube is a great resource for connecting with masters of a trade that you may not have the opportunity to encounter

in person, although you can utilize their knowledge in this form of learning, which is greatly helpful. This could be in the form a video series,
video course, or even a stand-alone video teaching you a single lesson
about a single topic.

- Pros:
  * Countless lessons and topics provided in video form
  * Interaction with the video publisher and viewers are possible
    through the comments section
  * The opportunity to learn and review at your own pace
  * No cost
- Cons:
  * YouTube may be unattainable for various reasons (internet
    access, devices, location, etc.)
  * The information is not always from a trustable source
  * The platform is not designed for education, which can recom-
    mend videos outside of your area of study
  * Because of the abundance of videos available, it can be difficult
    to find the video you need

Online Forums and Social Media   Online forums and social media for students discussing topics related to any trade have been growing
at an extremely rapid rate. The opportunity to post a question online
and receive an answer in seconds, along with the opportunity to teach
others who seek to learn what you know, can create a level of interaction
that is incredible for learning. There are many public and private groups
available both online and on social media platforms that are designed
specifically for students of music production, along with specific groups
that focus on a specific element of the process, such as song writing,
sound design, or mixing. These groups can be a great benefit to you as
a student who desires social interactions and a classroom setting in an
informal learning environment.

- Pros:
  * Builds motivation to grow through an enjoyable learning
    environment
  * Builds long-term skills through active learning

* Increases the opportunity to be both a teacher and student to others
* Cons:
    * Forums and social media may be unattainable for various reasons (internet access, devices, location, etc.)
    * The discussions and information are not always from a trustable source
    * Requires time for trial-and-error work to confirm results of the learning

Seminars and Webinars   Whether you're attending a trade show or you have enrolled in an online webinar, the opportunity to learn from an instructor, teacher, or master in the field of music production is in line with mentoring as a personal experience, if only for a short time. With the increase of live-streaming platforms, the number of seminars and webinars have grown so much that students have the ability to view and interact with some of their idols in real time—asking questions, receiving answers, and learning straight from the source.

* Pros:
    * Builds motivation to grow through an enjoyable learning environment
    * Builds long-term skills through active learning
    * Increases the opportunity to meet and discuss with masters of a trade
* Cons:
    * Seminars and webinars may be unattainable for various reasons (cost, time, devices, location, etc.)
    * With the abundance of webinars available, the presenter is not always a trustable source
    * Online events with no capacity limit may decrease your chances of interaction with the host

The Rule of Three

The "rule of three" means that there are three levels you can make use of when learning: those learning at a lower level than you, those who are your equals in learning and experience, and those having superior experience. Understanding your own current level will allow you to make use of these levels and congregate with these people to solidify your knowledge. Simply put, you can increase your knowledge by either learning from others, or learning on your own. An even better way to learn is to *teach*. By teaching others how to do something, you will learn more than you can imagine. Albert Einstein once said that the easier you can explain something, the better you know it. When you are teaching something to someone else, it's always best to make it as simple as you possible can. By doing so, you will learn the ins and outs of how something actually works. You will learn things you may not have thought of before you taught it to someone else. More importantly, if you don't know something well, you may be humiliated for a short time, and this is okay. Accepting this humility will allow you to learn about that topic in more depth. So, where does this all come into play?

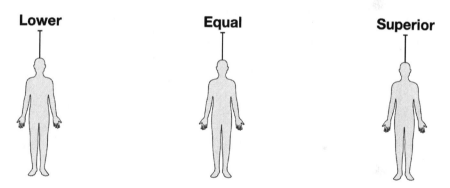

No matter what your level, there will always be people who are less experienced than you are, people at your own level, and people who are more experienced than you. It's very important to involve yourself with people at all three levels. There is a healthy balance of the three.

Lower Level: Teaching people who are at a lower level than you will increase your knowledge more than you may think. You being regarded as someone with experience will allow people to ask you questions that you may not have thought to ask. You may answer things in a way you haven't thought of before. Communicating and teaching those at a lower level is an incredible means of learning, not only for them, but you as well. Every time you explain or think about something you already know, you will be solidifying that idea into your long-term knowledge.

Equal Level: Communicating with people at your own level is incredibly important as well. You can gauge where others are in terms of their learning, you can learn what they are learning, and you can see how other people are making progress with things that you know, but they know slightly better. No matter how similar to others at this level you may be, there will always be topics for which you and other individuals differ. They might be better at one thing, while you are better at another. Seeing this and learning from this, and teaching them what you know, allows you to get the best of both worlds—as both a student and as a teacher to your associates.

Superior Level: Communicating with people and learning from those at a higher level is similar to taking part in mentorship. Learning the ins and outs of a subject and seeing how people at a higher level think and do things is not only inspiring, but incredibly helpful in showing you what works and what doesn't work. You may learn that some superiors are at a higher level in many aspects of production, but may be missing something of which you have more knowledge. For example, the best music producer in the world with more experience than you may not be a great song writer, and this may be something that you excel in. This doesn't mean you're better or worse than this person; it simply means that they have experience that makes them more prominent as a producer. Although you can learn from this producer in many ways, he or she may be able to learn some things from you as well. Although you may be able to teach something to these people, there will usually be a lot more that they can teach you. Remember: to your superiors, you are at a "lower level," meaning that they gain something from teaching you. Therefore, don't always feel like you are taking away from a superior's time by having them show you something, because in the end, they are gaining just as much as you are by teaching and growing on their own.

APPLICATION TO YOUR PRODUCTIONS

As a music producer of any level, it's very important to find a mentor to help shape the producer you will become, whether you believe this is important or not. This is a lesson I teach almost all of my own students.

I tell the students that I am not their only source for learning. I let them know that I am simply a single mentor to guide their path, in combination with other formal and informal methods of learning they can partake in. I often introduce my students to learning material not only from books, videos, and articles, but from other mentors as well. If my student needs to learn more in-depth techniques on mixing and mastering, I'll introduce them to an incredible mixing and mastering engineer with twenty-plus years of experience. I can introduce students to song writers with incredible success with hit songs, or I can introduce them to a mentor that can shape them in specific areas that I choose to not focus on myself. This is not only fine to do as both a student and a teacher, but it's incredibly healthy for both students and teachers to understand that there are multiple forms of learning available. The better we can interconnect this learning as a community and a culture, the greater the likelihood of building up our accumulated success as individuals.

For many of my students, it was difficult to understand when they would need a mentor and what subjects they should study or practice. Of course, if you're learning on your own, this is a difficult question, as your path for learning is usually constructed and guided by your mentors, *after* meeting them. Therefor it's important as a student of production learning on your own to understand how to gauge your own experience level, reflect on what you know, and reflect on what you do not understand. Doing this will give you an opportunity to choose a path for learning that will develop your growth as a producer, and will help you find a mentor to guide this path. Here's an exercise I share with many of my students, to allow them to make choices on what to learn outside of my mentorship, based on their own reflection regarding their current level of experience. Whenever my students hit a roadblock in their production workflow, they need to make a choice to overcome the roadblock with either formal or information learning. It sounds like a very simple concept, but it's something that is often overlooked, and it can be extremely helpful to take the time to gauge what you need to learn and how to learn it. For example, jumping into a YouTube playlist may not be the best scenario, but in another situations, YouTube may be your best option. Reflecting on what you need *before* jumping in may save you countless hours or even years of study, as you'll focus more on the learning you really need. This exercise is focused on:

1. Writing a goal
2. Writing a problem that created a roadblock to that goal
3. Writing two possible routes to fix this problem, either with formal or informal learning.

Let me show you a few examples of solving problems through formal, and informal learning to achieve your goal.

Goal: I want to produce and release my own original music.

1. **Problem:** I don't know anything about music theory.
    a. **Formal learning:** I want to attend a class on music theory.
    b. **Informal learning:** I want to learn through YouTube and friends who already produce music.
2. **Problem:** I'm terrible at synthesis sound design.
    a. **Formal learning:** I want to enroll in private lessons with a sound design teacher.
    b. **Informal learning:** I want to re-create my favorite songs through practice, until I figure it out.
3. **Problem:** I hate the way my mixes sound.
    a. **Formal learning:** I want to attend an audio engineering school.
    b. **Informal learning:** I want to become an intern at a studio and shadow a professional mixing engineer.

Exercise

For this exercise, write down at least a dozen things that you are saying or thinking as you facing an issue that is creating a roadblock in your production workflow, or something you imagine may be a future obstacle. Then, determine whether this is something you desire to solve with formal or informal learning. Write down what this desire would be. And finally, write who (or what) will handle the teaching. This is something you should be doing every day. I'm always looking for the questions and statements that I say or think as I decide how to move forward with my own personal growth. The truth is that most people don't see what the issues are until we stop, think, and reflect on them.

Exercise

My Goal: Release Original Music

Problem	Formal Learning	Informal Learning
I don't know music theory.	I want to attend a music theory class.	I want to learn from friends who already produce music.
I'm terrible at synth sound design.	I want to enroll in private sound design lessons.	I want to re-create my favorite songs and learn through practice.
I hate the way my mixes sound.	I want to attend an audio engineering school	I want to be an intern at a studio and learn through shadowing.

CONCLUSION

Tying It All Together

You now have an understanding of your role as a music producer and your music production process, and have reflected on your own order of preference, along with methods, concepts, and exercises to reflect on and develop as a producer. With this knowledge you are ready to move forward with your productions. I really hope this book has helped you with your understanding of music production. As mentioned earlier, this book has been created not just to help you learn from the exercises provided, but to be a stepping stone for your own future creation. Use the tips, tools, and approaches within this book to create the production you've always wanted, no matter where you currently are with your experience.

END NOTES

Here are some tips to help you get started with your new knowledge for music production.

Create a Calendar

In order to "get started," a calendar may be just the thing you need to jumpstart your journey. As a producer, setting a time frame for when you will *begin* and when you will *complete* a project may be the difference between starting in the first place, or not starting at all. Whether you're into using a paper notepad, or you prefer a digital calendar, utilizing a system to visualize an overview of your year, your month, your week, and even your days can be a useful adjustment for moving your output in a consistent upward direction.

Time-Based Sprints

In order to complete your tasks, you have the option of deciding completion based on the quality of your content or based on the time spent on your content. A useful habit to apply to your production can be setting weekly or even daily time-based sprints (e.g., one or two hours per day) to work on a specific aspect of your production, and move the following sprint to where you left off. This is a process that can allow you to gauge how much you are capable of achieving in a specific amount of time, and can easily lead you to focusing more effort on achieving results within this time sprint, as opposed to thinking you have all the time in the world to achieve a goal.

When you become aware of and comfortable with the amount of work you can achieve within your chosen sprint time, you can advance to limiting specific processes in your projects to a certain amount of time, leading to a realistic deadline for completion.

Experiment and Try New Things

All of the information and exercises in this book are great additions to your own personal knowledge, although there are no rules saying that these are the only ways to produce music. Have fun with your own process, and try things that you haven't seen in this book or heard anywhere else in the world. Who knows? That could be the new sound you've been looking for all along.

Further Explore Music

A very important but easy way to understand various styles of music is simply to listen to them. Whether you are a personal fan of electronic dance music, rock, jazz, hip-hop, funk, or any other styles, try expanding your musical vocabulary by listening to music you are not familiar with. There is a very good chance that this will open you up to a new understanding and appreciation of different styles. Hearing new styles of music, and listening to productions in these styles, will help you understand the sound, feel, and application of concepts you've learned in this book, which will greatly benefit your music production workflow.

Explore Creators

Just as important as listening to music is discovering who was involved with this music. The more you learn about the creators of the productions you are hearing, the more you will understand the craft and industry as a whole. The music production world is more a lifestyle than an occupation, and the more you know about the people within this community, the more opportunities you will have to relate to, communicate with, and collaborate with these creators that you may even aspire to meet some day.

If you hear a song with a mixdown that you love, find out who mixed it. If you hear a song with an absolutely killer bass line, find out who played it. The more you understand the craft, and the more you understand the people involved, the more opportunities will open for you. Many creators, even the ones at "the top," may be humbled by your appreciation of their own creations, and welcome you into this community based purely on your love, dedication, and interest in the art of music production.

INDEX

solution, 21, 24, 33–34, 43–44, 50–
  51, 70–71, 103, 105–7, 109, 111,
  113–14, 121
sound design, 13, 15–18, 20–21, 24–
  25, 27–29, 31–33, 38–40, 46–50,
  55–56, 62, 73–81, 83–87, 90–91,
  108, 115–16, 125, 130
sound designer, 15, 18, 21, 28,
  33, 50, 55–56, 76–78, 85–86,
  116
soundscape, 29, 31, 33

song writer, 21, 33, 47, 50, 56, 58, 61,
  63, 69–71, 77, 116, 128–29
song writing, 13, 25–26, 28, 32–33,
  38–40, 46–50, 55–59, 61, 63–65,
  67, 69, 70–71, 74, 98, 106, 115–16,
  125
synthesizer, 21, 40, 47, 50, 77, 80–81

taste, 12, 14, 30, 44, 119
timbre, 27–29, 33, 43, 47, 76, 78–79,
  81–82

ABOUT THE AUTHOR

Josh Bess is a music producer, educator, and author from New York. Working with the Hal Leonard Corporation, Bess is the author of the popular music book *Electronic Dance Music Grooves* and has created multiple TEC Award–nominated instructional video courses. He is an artist and producer with releases through Armada Music; a music producer at Amazon Fashion Week Tokyo; and a studio drummer with multiple television and commercial music placements on MTV, Disney, and Nickelodeon networks. He has also worked for years as an educator of electronic music creation. Backed by these diverse experiences, Bess has the expertise to understand the goals and strengthen the skills of aspiring artists and producers within this creative industry.

In addition to his experience, Bess demonstrates his knowledge and passion for education as an Ableton Certified Trainer with Ableton, and holding a Higher Education Teaching Certificate with Harvard University. These two certifications signify Bess's in-depth understanding of the software and instruments he uses to create music, along with his deep passion for teaching and learning to encourage his students' motivation, performance, and growth as creators in the music industry.